Testimony

A collection of stories of how Jesus has changed peoples lives.

Gathered by Ruby Smith

Hey there,

I am so glad this book is in your hands. Like... I'm so glad!
This is not a traditional kinda book (which is fun!)
It's a book you can pick up at any point and not feel like you
have forgotten the story (wahoo!)
Each page is a different story and testimony of faith from
someone around the world.
How cool is that!

Throughout this book, there are stories of redemption, healing,
restoration, prayers being answered, joyful moments and hard
moments. I encourage you to read them slowly and ask the Holy
Spirit to fill you and speak to you as you read.

I want you to know that you are so loved by Jesus.
He has a beautiful plan for your life.
That's not to say the Christian life is an easy ride - it's a
tough one - but I believe it's the best one.
If you don't have a relationship with Jesus yet, that's okay.
I encourage you as you read this book to have an open heart and
allow yourself to be impacted by each testimony.

Have a good day,
Ruby

Many of the Samaritans from that town believed in him because of the woman's testimony.

John 4:39

My Testimony

I knew Jesus but I didn't know him. I had a secret habit… an eating disorder. When lockdown 2020 came, everything was heightened - my thoughts, habits and exercise. Everything was out of control so instead of running to Jesus, I restricted food and excessively exercised as a coping mechanism as this was the only thing that I could control. I became totally obsessed with myself and how I looked. I started to weigh myself and the number became who I was. The number started to go down but I became more anxious and sad. My clothes became too big so I was ordering smaller clothes that weren't meant to fit me.

When meal times came I was not fun to be around, my shoulders would go up and my body would become very rigid as all I was thinking about was calories, calories, calories and how I would have to go on a run in the morning to burn it all off. Most nights I would go through in my mind what I had eaten that day and this would affect whether I was happy with myself or not. This led to spiralling thoughts of, "I should not have eaten that…why did I?" or, "I'm so proud of myself for not having those chocolates". I was totally exhausted every day from the same repetitive thoughts, and looking back now I can see why I was so tired and ready for bed at 6pm.

Planning meals became a massive part of the control. One night, I had worked out what I wanted to eat the next day, so I walked to the kitchen and took bacon out of the freezer at 10pm, and then at 7:30am the next day I walked to my local Tescos to buy lettuce for my BLT wrap. All I thought about was what, when, how much I would eat next and when I would go on my next run.

There was one particular morning when I was done, done with

Ruby, UK

My Testimony

the loud thoughts, done with it all. I decided to bring it into the light. So I walked out of my room and I saw my mum and told her that I was struggling with eating and exercising. I am forever grateful for my mum, she held and prayed for me as I sobbed into her arms, and ever since that morning, she has continued to encourage, champion and challenge me. After that moment I wasn't healed from the eating disorder, it became even harder as we had to deal with a lot of the thoughts and habits that I had kept hidden for such a long time. I began to tell people outside my family circle - I really wanted my close family and friends to know so that I could take them on my journey of learning to love food again. I didn't want everyone to know as it was still quite raw but needed to have people who I could chat about it with at any point.

Throughout this season I had never felt the nearness of Jesus so closely and strongly. My worship has become so different. The line in one of my favourite songs says, "I'm no longer a slave to fear" and I truly believe what I am singing. I was a slave to this eating disorder but because of Jesus, I am becoming more and more free every day. It's a battle every day but I'm getting there and it's no longer a battle that I face on my own…I do it with Jesus. I wake up every morning and I have to choose what voice I am going to listen to; the enemy's voice or God's voice. I feel so beautiful. I love food now and I exercise not to burn calories but to look after my body.

Thank you, Jesus.

Ruby, UK

I've had 3 rounds of IVF and gone through 11 miscarriages and never had my own baby. My husband asked me every year what I would like for my birthday and I always said a baby. We decided to adopt 9 years ago and began going through the process. We got a call one day to say a baby boy had been born addicted to heroin and they thought he would be perfect for us... We met him... On my birthday!!!!!!!!

We then decided to adopt a second time. Went through the process again, waited for over a year and nothing happened. I sat down in tears one evening and told my husband I'd given up hope. I thought it was never going to happen. I had zero hope left. The next day we got a call… A baby girl has been born addicted to heroin and they thought she would be perfect for us... Oh, and by the way, her name is 'Hope'.

We decided we were happy with two children - life was full and busy! It was coming up to my birthday again and we got a call saying our son's birth mum was about to give birth again and the baby would need to be adopted, would we do it again? We said yes! And I got our third and final baby...on my birthday! God has been incredibly good and kind to us!!

Clare, UK

I grew up a Muslim and stayed a Muslim for a few years after I graduated high school. After that, I started having doubts about the religion I was brought up in. For a while, I didn't outwardly profess these doubts and still called myself a Muslim. Inwardly, I knew that I didn't believe in the divinity of the Quran.

Eventually, I admitted that I was an atheist, not believing in anything. That led to a long, dark road for me. Partying, heavy drinking and deep depression for many years. On the worldly side, I started my PhD in 2015 and completed it in December 2019. I did not immediately have a job lined up after this and the busyness of the PhD was gone. That led up to a very dark night in February 2020 when I attempted to take my own life. That night was the darkest night of my life. After not wanting to live for so many years, my worst nightmare had come true: I was stuck in this world whether I wanted to or not.

After a lot of drinking, I remember that in my really intoxicated state, I called out, "God, if you're there, I need you." The next day, I woke up with a terrible migraine from a hangover. In the evening, I decided to go for a walk (since I was unemployed and had really nothing to do). During that walk, I realised that, for the first time in so many years, I just wanted to live. I just didn't want to go to sleep wishing I didn't wake up, and to those who have been in the abyss of depression, feeling that for the first time in so long is by far the best feeling that anyone can experience!

So, within a short span of 24 hours, I realised that my whole belief in atheism had been wrong this entire time. Clearly, there was a higher being out there, but I had no idea who he was. That led to a spiritual search that lasted a few weeks. I looked into

Kaab, Pakistan

Islam and other religions. Coming from a Muslim background, I didn't look into Christianity because I thought I already knew everything about Jesus. But, after not finding spiritual truth in any of the other religions that I looked into, I decided to investigate Christianity as the last resort. I googled some stuff and eventually, I landed on a video of a preach at a conference. The speaker was talking about many things - most of which went over my head at the time. But what struck me was the scripture he was quoting; John 3:16, Genesis 1 and Matthew 5:16. By the end of the talk I knew in my heart that this was it… this was the truth. I got down on my knees and prayed directly to Jesus Christ and accepted Him as my Lord and Saviour for the first time ever.

Praying to him was the best thing ever - the internal peace that experienced was unlike anything else. That's how I became a Christian. As for the rest of my story, through a unique set of circumstances, I was able to land a job. I moved and started going to a church, I established myself in a great community and I have made awesome friends. I have grown in my faith and I continue to grow. I'm grateful to God for bringing me here, and for hearing my cry for help that fateful night. I have faltered many times since then in pursuing Him - many, many times. But at the end of the day, I know He loves me unconditionally and keeps embracing me with open arms. That's my message to anyone else who's on the fence about the Bible or Jesus. Jesus loves you. Put your faith in Him and you will not regret it.

I am so peaceful with Jesus in my life. I love bringing him into every part of my life, when I'm doing something mundane to stressful situations, I create conversation prayers to let him into my life and it creates such peace.

Jess, UK

My mum was diagnosed with breast cancer. At that point, I was a Christian by name only but I remember just before we got the results, I was home alone in the kitchen and I broke down sobbing (to this day I've never cried like that) and I begged God not to make my mum go through that. I remember saying something like, "if you're real, show me!". There's no mega turnaround here because my mum did get cancer and I was so angry with God - I was so uninterested in Him or church or Christianity.

I was convinced everyone was serving a super mean, awful guy who loved to punish and ignore people's sadness. At that time I also really struggled with anxiety and depression and I was just really lost in my misery. I put on a brave face for my mum but I really didn't see the point of living and each day was such a battle. I was also doing important exams so everything felt like it was swallowing me whole from all angles! That whole season of my life is a bit of a blur.

But the turning point was when it all got too much and carrying all that hurt and anger was doing nothing for me. At our church youth gathering, I received prayer to have a fresh start - it wasn't something instant but I slowly felt myself letting go more and more, and each day I felt lighter and I made the choice to not carry that anymore.

I was also so encouraged by my mum who every morning before her treatment would blast her worship music and praise God and I just thought if she still believes God is good and she's the one that's ill, it's not for me to carry anger on her behalf. I'm sure my family saw through my act and prayed so hard for me, and as I also prayed, I slowly turned back to God.

Sandra, Zimbabwe

I think the moment my faith finally became mine was in Lock-down 1.0 when I had so much time and so little to do - I just dove right into my bible, fell in love with the Lord's presence and just went from there. I spent hours with Jesus and he became my best friend. Of course, it hasn't been a linear journey and there's still growing left to do but I'm so happy with how far I've come already! I honestly believe if Jesus hadn't saved my life, I don't know if I would be alive and well today and I have never regretted the moment I decided he would be my friend.

Honestly, going through all that was hard but now, looking back, I can see God was always present in every part and I wouldn't change a thing about my story! I can promise you that reading this, even when you can't see him, God is in the details and your miracle won't always look like a grand gesture from heaven. For me, the miracle wasn't my mum's cancer disappearing but it was the fact that she survived and is so happy and healthy now!!

Sandra, Zimbabwe

When I was four I started and fell in love with soccer - sorry I know it's offensive for me to call it that but it helps me because I get confused with American football. Anyways, I fell in love with the game and it became my one true love in life. I went to church and grew up in a family that was adamant about being involved in church, but I never cared.

In my 8th-grade year, I had a tumour on my knee which had to be removed. I then had surgery which shouldn't have taken too long to recover from but for some unknown reason, it took longer than expected. Once I got back to soccer I was playing in a tournament and I tore my ACL and meniscus in the last game. This was a life-changing moment for me because it took the very thing that I loved. It wrecked me to the core. This happened about five games after I got back from my other injury. I got so depressed and hated my life so much, pushed my friends away and just was so empty.

That's when I started searching for something more. I knew Christianity because of my history in the church so I started elsewhere, I started looking into UFOs. I then got tired of this and moved on to government conspiracies and deeper stuff like that, but it never fulfilled me. I then went to the other main religions of the world. I researched Islam, Hinduism, Buddhism, Judaism, and eventually Christianity.

I started to read the Bible. I tried so hard to prove it wrong, to find fallacies in it or anything I could. I found nothing that I could prove against it. During this time I discovered the Bible is true.

Once, at work, it was a really rough day, afterwards my boss and

Will, USA

I were just sitting and talking, when all of a sudden the Holy Spirit fell on me! I then got plugged into a church and started to serve and gain more responsibility.

I am now a young adult pastor and the creative director at the church I work at. It's been a ride but the Lord has been so faithful to see me through. God also poured His Spirit out and showed me the world through His lens. I no longer hate people or long for truth, my soul is fulfilled now. I treat others with care, I desire to love people. God freed me from deep anger problems. My personality is new, I feel much more joyful and intentional. I am no longer depressed, I have my moments but God always draws me out of them. I am free!

When I was 11 I was diagnosed with Idiopathic Scoliosis (curvature of the spine), and at the age of 12 I had major spinal surgery which left me with PTSD, chronic pain and fatigue. My life went from school, drawing and playing with my younger brother to hospital appointments in London, MRI scans and unbelievable pain. It jolted life for me and my family completely.

After a number of different unusual and mostly extremely painful treatments, I was told that I needed spinal surgery. I was hoping that this would be the case, as I wanted Scoliosis to be done with so I could move on with my life. I had experienced bullying and exclusion at my primary school and after many prayers for good friendships, I had made a good group of friends at secondary school, so things seemed on the up - little did I know what I was in for. I endured 12-hour neurosurgery and I now have 11 titanium screws in my spine - I was heavily sedated for days, and spent two days alone in ICU. I had two chest drains and one lumbar drain which leaked out disgusting-looking liquid from my body, I lost 2st 1lb in a day and all I wanted was my mum. I went from a confident, smiley average 12-year-old girl to a sick trying-to-stay-positive-but-dying-inside young girl. I experienced more pain in one week than anybody might experience in a lifetime. I was away from school so much that I lost my friends, my relationship with my family had completely changed and I became a different person.

Over two years later in 2020, I was hit by a deep wave of trauma from my experience - I grieved the person I was before my surgery, and hated the person I was after. I stopped going to church and my faith really started to decline. I felt like I had lost my childhood. For so many years I had been robbed by chronic pain, fatigue, depression and PTSD. I still shudder to think about

Sasha, UK

the whole experience. I'd like to say that Jesus pulled me out of it in one swift motion and I was immediately okay, but over time I realised that Jesus was with me the whole time. Ever since he created me in my mother's womb, he has been with me. He was with me in the ICU when I was alone. He was with me when I felt suicidal on my bedroom floor. He was with me when I felt the most alone I've ever felt as I screamed by the bathroom sink. He's with me on my best days, with me on my worst days, and every day in between.

Eventually, I felt so terrible mentally and physically that I wanted to drop out of school after my first important exam because I was in too much pain to continue. I would pretend to people I knew, such as my friends, teachers and people at church that I was completely fine after four years post-surgery, but I was so desperate for help that I genuinely wanted to be hospitalised at 16.

I was prescribed Codeine by my GP but I only took it when I went to bed as it made me extremely nauseous and sleepy, which was obviously not ideal for school! I felt like such a burden to my family and friends as I was always ill and sad, even thinking about how rough that time was makes me tearful.

I'd like to say that I felt better immediately after therapy, medication and prayer and that I was okay, but it took months for me to feel like myself again. I started to laugh more often and really enjoy the food. I started cooking and baking, I read my novels and spent more time in our garden, I started going back to church and I ventured out of the house more than I did before.

Although I was expecting low grades from my important exam

Sasha, UK

results (as I was ill throughout the exam season), I managed to pass all exams with all A's and B's, and one A* for Art which I was so happy with! Instead of leaving school with one result (which was the plan), I left with seven. God really helped me reach the light at the end of the tunnel.

I've never forgotten what one person said on a post on Instagram maybe a few years ago, "You have no idea what God has saved you from." That has always stuck with me. God has saved me from death, destruction and depression so many times. I see it even more clearly every time I look back to that dark period, and see God was with me, especially through the love of the people around me and the protection of His angels surrounding me every day.

I still struggle with my faith and my health, but now that I have put my life in God's hands fully and completely I am so excited to see what He has in store for me. If you're reading this and you're going through a tough mental or physical health period, just trust in God that you'll get through it. It could be weeks, months or years, it could take therapy and medication, but you will get through it.

God bless, Sasha.

When I was about 11, I fell from the top of a bouldering wall (5-6m high without a harness) and jarred both of my ankles really badly. This resulted in having pain in one or both ankles very regularly, to the point that on a couple of occasions I was in a wheelchair for about a year. I had been pain-free for about a month, assuming the physiotherapy was working.

I went to a youth festival and one of the evenings it was a 'healing night', and as this was mentioned I collapsed in agony. The youth from the group I was with, who did not know me as I was there at a friend's church, gathered around me and began to pray. Within half an hour, I was not only able to stand but to walk, run, jump and dance, completely pain-free. 8 years later, I am still pain-free! God hears our prayers, no matter our age, and He is still in the miracle-working business!!!

Anna, UK

What was life like before you met Jesus?

Silent.

Pretty depressing, Dark and Suicidal.

It was so miserable!! I was battling depression and anxiety and finding temporary solutions in all the wrong places and I just never knew true freedom and Joy.

A mess, and very insecure, looked to toxic relationships, drugs, and alcohol to satisfy the deep longings I had.

I was constantly searching for the approval of the people around me and I was pretty empty and bitter as a result.

A mix of fun and disappointment but overall meaningless and I had a lack of confidence.

It was empty, Things that I thought were fun were just things leaving me empty and lost.

Very self-fulfilling, I was very grumpy all the time and had no joy or hope.

Dark, lonely, anxiety-inducing, uncertain and hopeless.

Empty, hard to understand, shallow and very troubled.

It was dark, unsettling and overall a bit stale!

Full of me, full of my sorrows and full of my past.

Full of comparison which stole all my joy.

Multiple people

What was life like before you met Jesus?

Religious and stale.

Difficult.

Selfish.

I can only think of it as beige, it wasn't an awful life but it didn't have the vivid colour I see it as now. I was happy but didn't know true Joy or what purpose felt like!

Boring and lonely.

Fake and empty.

Out of control.

It lacked meaning and purpose, and I struggled a lot with anxiety and social anxiety which I believe greatly has improved since giving my life to Jesus.

It was dark and empty.

Completely colourless. I was extremely depressed, confused about who I was, constantly searching for validation, broken and in need of something real and genuine.

Pretty confusing, full of not-great decisions and self-hatred.

There was a void only Jesus could fill.

I lived for the approval of others and my value was found in what others thought of me.

Multiple people

Growing up, I never truly understood what having a relationship with Jesus looked like or what it meant. I didn't know what I needed to be saved from, but being in Sunday school, I learnt many things.

My childhood was speckled with the habit of masturbation. It wasn't something I didn't know a lot about except the fact that it felt good and it made me feel things I had never felt before. This discovery brought a mixture of feelings: shame, guilt, pleasure and conviction. I began to hide and became secretive about it. I fell into this pit on and off throughout my childhood and teen years. When I was 13, I stumbled upon a porn magazine while at a friend's place. I was mortified at what I saw and felt coated in shame and guilt all over again but this time with an intensity I hadn't felt. I felt dirty. Exposed. Filthy. Yet I'd return to it. But one day, I'd had enough. I wanted it gone.

So I decided to do something about it. I went back only to discover that partial remains of the magazine had been left behind. Without wanting anyone else to see what I'd seen, I took the liberty of setting the remaining pieces of the magazine on fire. I didn't think it would affect me later in life, but it did.

I thank God for placing people into my life when I needed them and how He orchestrated moments in my life that would help change my life forever.

I became increasingly aware of my desperate need for a saviour when I was 15 years old. I began to seek God out after having attended Bible studies on my lunch breaks at work. A friend decided to take it upon herself to enrol me in a Bible study correspondence where I'd receive weekly teachings in the mail for me

Trudy, Canada

to fill out and send back. The girls in this lunch study inspired me to read scripture, worship, pray and seek God. A friend asked me one day if I had accepted Jesus and I said no. That conversation led to many more and an opening for God to move in me.

Being honest with yourself is hard and being honest with myself and acknowledging the fact that I didn't have a relationship with God was uncomfortable, to say the least. I wrestled with surrender. A friend from the study began to write me letters encouraging me to follow Jesus and helping me understand that following Jesus was worth it.

In my quest to seek God out, an undoing of lies upon lies, of religion, of rules I'd heard my whole life began to take place in my heart. In the midst of this seeking, questioning, crying out to God, journalling time, fear crept in and was insistent on making its home in me. Fear that carried dread, gloom, a heaviness that left me unable to breathe properly. It physically made me feel crippled.

Even when suicide crossed my mind, He didn't allow it to come to fruition. Even when I was so depressed, He never left me. Even when I wanted nothing to do with anyone, He was still by my side. Even when I cried myself to sleep almost every night, He remained close. Even when I didn't recall how I managed to survive days, weeks and months, He carried me throughout it all.

When I was 17, I met Jesus in a bathroom at a chiropractor's appointment. With my face down in the hole of the massage table, she asked me if I wanted to receive Christ (lol). At first, I avoided the question. But I couldn't avoid it the second time, I said

Trudy, Canada

yes. Yes, I wanted to accept Jesus. I don't remember what she prayed over me that day but I do know that I made my way to the bathroom and bawled and bawled and asked Jesus into my life.

I experienced a joy and a peace I hadn't known before. There was peace in my soul regarding the future, about my present, about my decision. That crippling fear I had many encounters with disappeared; it vanished. I felt new. I felt alive. I felt hope. I felt courageous.

To all the prayers people prayed over me, to all the countless hours where I listened to worship, all the journaling, and all the lunch break Bible studies that turned into crying and worshipping. To all the people who walked alongside me, who helped pull me out of my comfort zones, who pushed me, encouraged me, wept with me, laughed with me, held me, took the time to help me understand the things of God.

What a work of God. I'm so thankful. The moments in between when I thought I was ruined because of my exposure to a porn magazine, when I thought I had to hide instead of boldly coming before the throne of God.

I'm still learning that God is able to take on the questions that seem profound and deeply confusing to me; He's able to take on my hurt, my anger, my disappointments, and my frustrations. Had it not been for the pull of God on my heart and imperfect, messy, wholesome relationships with imperfect people, I'd not be here today.

Praise the Lord!

Trudy, Canada

I know He is with me all the time. I don't live with the anxiety that would normally consume my thoughts and debilitate me from doing anything purposeful. I no longer despise myself when I make mistakes. He rescued me from me, from the enemy and from the lies.

Simone, South Africa

We were in the thick of raising our four young children on one salary. We were very content but finances were a struggle. In 2016, we attended a conference and had the opportunity to sign up for a prophecy session. It was there that a lady said to me, 'I have a sense that God wants to give you something back, that you feel you have lost'. She continued, 'I see you standing at the edge of the sea and you throw something into the water. What comes back in the waves is greater than you ever imagine and God is going to give back to you abundantly. The sense I have is that this is a 'painting gift'.

Motherhood was so all-encompassing. My husband and I were also leading our church and pastoring others, and this meant there was little time for me to create. I'd always loved creating, but I wasn't a painter.

Nine months after the prophecy was given, my friend asked me to join her in exhibiting artwork at a local art house. I remember laughing at the absurdity of producing anything worthy of public viewing. However, I agreed. I had no idea what or how I'd paint but I bought some oil paints and canvases and started painting. That evening, I painted a few seascapes and as I painted the waves, I remembered the prophecy from nine months earlier.

The exhibition was interesting. My friend had painted huge skulls and I painted wistful seascapes. It was the strangest collaboration! I was amazed that people bought my paintings. The following year I was invited back for a solo exhibition and it was here that a lady cried in front of a stormy painting. God was speaking to her about Him being a Creator.

Over the years, God has continued to use my creativity and has

Esther, UK

spoken prophetically about the homes in which the paintings will end up. I remember one time, God spoke to me about a particular painting that I was working on. It was going to a family who had lost several babies and they had made the decision to stop IVF. In my mind, as I prayed and painted, I could see them with another child. I named the painting 'Hope'.

You can imagine my squeal when I heard, several months later, that they had conceived naturally. The pregnancy went well and they now have a gorgeous son! God has indeed given back to me.

Esther, UK

When I was 12 years old I became super sick with a ton of different health issues including chronic Lyme disease. I was bed bound, homebound and had doctors telling me there wasn't much they could do to help me beat it.

One night the Lord spoke to me and told me that He was my Healer and He was going to heal my body and my mind (from emotional hurts related). I was completely healed that night and set on fire for Jesus. I began to preach and tell people about the way He healed me and because of it, the Lord called me into the medical field. He is the most faithful and He is more beautiful and more worthy and better than I ever thought possible.

Megan, USA

I was diagnosed with clinical depression at age 14, after facing some trauma within my school and personal life. The trauma caused me to feel unloved every second of my life. I saw the world through a black and white filter, not wanting to be alive or receive help.

We had an assembly in school where we were all given a little book of the New Testament, but as a young girl who's only focus was the thought of not living anymore, I forgot about the book I'd been given and just put it on a shelf. One time I'd finished crying in my room and I had an overwhelming thought that I should read through this book - that something in there might give me that ounce of hope to carry on. I must have read about two pages and those intrusive thoughts returned to me again. The thought of Jesus crossed my mind in the following years, knowing that if anything ever got extremely bad, the Bible would be my last resort.

At the age of 16 I started smoking cigarettes, weed and vaping, doing everything I could to fill that void, but it never quite filled it completely. When I reached 18 I was still in a dark place, in a mindset where I didn't think anything could end the pain. I was scrolling through Instagram and I came across a song called, 'I Surrender' which I thought was beautifully written and sung; the artist seemed to have so much passion. I added it to my playlist and it would keep popping up when I would shuffle it. It wasn't until a few months after that I found myself laying on my bed with this song that had randomly started playing again. No song had ever made me feel so at peace and so heard. Jesus then became a recurring thought, maybe once or twice a week.

I moved to uni shortly after this and on a Sunday in September

Eleanor, UK

at about 5 pm, I was laying on my bed watching the sun go down. I went downstairs to get to know my housemates and we were thinking about what to do. One of my housemates turned to me and said, "just so you know, I'm a Christian, we could go down to Church as they have late-night worship tonight." I was quickly reminded of that evening when I lay in bed wondering what life was about. I said, 'I'd love to go' and off we went to church.

That evening, I wondered why on earth I was spending my first evening at uni in a church when I could've been down on the beach smoking a pack of cigarettes and watching the sunset. But something felt so right about what I was doing instead. As I walked into the church, I could hear this singing voice and instruments, it just hit me like a ton of bricks and I felt so much excitement. I walked in and as I took my first steps, something sounded familiar.

There was a girl and a band standing beneath a lit-up cross surrounded by worshippers singing, "I Surrender." At that moment I just knew this wasn't a coincidence, out of the thousands of worship songs, that was the one that was being sung. This beautiful voice just sang a song that connected with me so much. The rest was history, I went to that church every night that I could and joined the student community.

That first student night, I walked in on my own so so nervous that I wasn't worthy to be there because of all the things I had done in my life. It was the same girl with her guitar and a few blankets and cushions on the floor. It was so intimate and I felt ready to just surrender everything to Jesus. She started singing and I opened myself up completely within a matter of minutes.

Eleanor, UK

I was on my knees sobbing, trying everything I could to keep it in so people wouldn't see but it was so uncontrollable.

Shortly after, I felt this overwhelming sense of peace, ten times bigger than ever before and I just stayed in that place with Jesus and imagined myself resting on Him and falling asleep in His arms. That night that had gone on for three hours went by so fast, I wasn't ready to leave that place with the Lord. It was something I had never felt in my life and that's when I knew that I wanted that feeling and experience over and over again. I realised that I could have that if I gave my life to Him and followed him and let Him guide me.

Within a week, the need for a cigarette or any type of drug had just completely disappeared, and since then I haven't touched any of it. I am forgiven, I am loved. I am reminded every single day that He saw me in those times when I had nothing left, He saw me in those hopeless moments when I was crying every single day and it wasn't until the first encounter that I realised He had a plan for me all along and He was going to save me and live in me for the rest of my life.

Eleanor, UK

I've learned that He truly still works miracles today. In the fall of 2021, I hurt my knee while playing sports. I was in pain for a long time and I didn't know what was wrong. One night during a youth group, I was praying for healing for my knee. After the youth group was done, I went down on my knee to see if the pain was still there. I felt the Holy Spirit's presence as I realised there was no more pain!!

Abigail, USA

Probably the biggest struggle I've experienced in my life was when I was around 13 years old. As a young teenage girl, I was curious and ended up watching pornography. This was easily the darkest time in my life. I couldn't stop watching it and it was something I couldn't avoid, I knew it wasn't right but I would always go back to it. I carried a lot of shame as I was so young and the struggle with addiction was something very hard to overcome.

I was able to turn to Jesus after I realised that it wasn't right and was causing a lot of hurt and shame in my life. Jesus swooped in and forgave me and I've been able to heal since this time. It was hard and I still feel embarrassed about it but I know that this is what millions of young people, even Christians, struggle with behind closed doors today. I've learned that Jesus's love is the only love that will truly satisfy me. This has been a huge barrier in my life, but I'm happy to have come out of it and now can mentor younger girls struggling with this kind of sin. I think that girls struggling with pornography addictions are not addressed enough, especially in Christian circles, so I think it's really important to talk about it!!

Ava, New Zealand

I was a teen runaway. I ran from an abusive and neglectful home at the age of 16. I lived a nomadic life peddling drugs and struggling with addiction. When I was 21, I fell in love with a girl who invited me to church. It was an intercession prayer service, not a simple church service. I encountered the Holy Spirit that night. I walked free from addiction, married my girlfriend and within two years was in training for ministry.

There have been so many changes over the 25 years since that night. The biggest impact has been the breaking of generational poverty and addiction. Jesus brought me new life, purpose and direction. In that process, He broke poverty from my life, and my three children have benefitted from God's faithfulness and blessing.

There's knowing Him as my Father. I never knew my biological father, and my life was overwhelmed with abandonment and rejection. His love is unconditional. I didn't deserve for Him to meet me with love and salvation that night. The outside appearance and the behaviours aren't what he finds when He comes to us. He knows the brokenness of our hearts and that's why He comes.

William, USA

Growing up, the idea of God wasn't even on my radar. When I was 17 years old, I was invited to a Friday youth group at a church by a guy I was chatting with at the time… Yep, I started going to church for a guy but now I go to church for Jesus!

Anyway, I started attending and serving at youth regularly. A month after going to church there was a youth weekend event I attended. During the last talk on Saturday evening, the speaker locked eye contact with me and said, "You are loved. You are chosen. You are called to make a difference." At that moment my eyes began to well up and I felt something move in my heart. Later that night I decided to live my life for Jesus and invited Him into my life. The best decision I've ever made.

Life hasn't been the easiest, but I know God wants to use every bit of it to help draw others closer to Him. Growing up, my mum had some severe mental illnesses and my dad worked ridiculous hours to help look after us and provide for us financially. I love them both sooo much! They're amazing parents. But this meant that a lot of the time growing up I helped look after my mum (since the age of 5), whilst my dad was at work. Despite how sometimes my childhood was tough, scary and dark, my experiences helped me develop a heart for helping others. The amazing thing is that since coming to faith I can look back and see that God was with me in every single moment. In the lowest of the lows and highest of the highs. That he always has and always will be with me.

When I was 16 I started to struggle with my own mental health. It deteriorated really quickly. Within the space of four months, I went from feeling anxious and depressed to struggling with my eating and self-harming, to several near-suicide attempts. Since

Jodie, UK

coming to faith it has completely changed my perspective on life. It gives me hope. A hope that this world can never take away because it's found in the One who never changes and is ever-lasting. A hope that's found and embodied in our friend Jesus, our living hope.

The first few years of following Jesus have also been super tough. In the first four months I was in an abusive relationship with my boyfriend (the guy who invited me to church). During that time, my Grandma was re-diagnosed with cancer. On the same day, my boyfriend broke up with me and my Grandma passed away. That was a really tough time, especially being new to faith as well. At first, I thought I was coping quite well but I later became quite mentally ill because of it. I had been in denial of the sexual abuse that was going on. When I finally realised what had happened I started to really struggle with my faith. I dropped out of college and was feeling suicidal again. One night I was crying to God not knowing what to do with my life, feeling like I couldn't go on anymore. Then I felt like I heard God say (the clearest I've ever heard from Him), "focus on how I saw you before time began". No one had ever said that to me but it filled a desire in me to find out how God saw me before time began.

I then spent the following two weeks constantly looking at scripture, doing research, praying and reflecting on what I came across. I went back to God saying, "wow, thank you so much for guiding me with this, thank you that since before time began I have been loved, known and chosen by you. But okay I understand you saw me like that before time began, but what does that mean for today? For right here and now"? I felt God say, "What I spoke over you before the creation of Heaven and Earth I will

Jodie, UK

continue to speak over you for eternity. Because I am Love and my love endures forever." Hearing this from God has helped me get through some really dark times. I can't thank God enough! That God didn't just start loving me when I started loving Him, but He has loved me since before time began, since before I was born, and will love me into eternity and nothing can change that.

Jodie, UK

I was extremely anxious and worried a lot of the time which made me very fearful for the future. I would feel sick before going to school and cry multiple times whilst at school. I was overridden with anxiety and it made me feel like there was no hope as I couldn't see how I would be able to leave home ever or do anything outside of my comfort zone. After I received prayer at a festival I felt so at peace and ever since then Jesus has led me on a wonderful journey of overcoming the worry I felt on a daily basis. Don't get me wrong it still feels painful at times but my outlook has completely changed because I have a friend in Jesus who has a plan for my life.

Hannah, UK

About a decade ago, my family experienced the power of Jesus. You see, at the time my family were Hindu and it was a ritual to light the God lamp. This specific evening as my mom was lighting the God lamp, my sister ended up collapsing out of the blue. My dad was scared, so he started calling on all the Hindu God's, but my sister didn't respond until one of the most powerful moments of our life… Our neighbour at the time started to pray and call upon Jesus. At that moment she responded.

Sharnay, South Africa

My family has experienced immense suffering. However, with each ounce of brokenness I've felt, Jesus has rescued me and healed me. He's shown up in ways I could never possibly have fathomed.

I have been fatherless, experienced loneliness, and watched my family suffer from poor mental health and suicide, yet I have witnessed friends being physically healed and saved.

I've encountered God in my weakness. God has answered prayers and held me close. He's saved me and called me His own. I have hope. I can rest on Him and in Him. I can honestly say my understanding of love has massively grown. Not only do I know the love He has for me, but also the call we have to love His world and His people.

God has protected me and lifted me out of the darkness and re-placed it with joy. My story reflects something of God's faithful-ness to his children. Life still leaves bruises but I know God is with me. God has called me to work and lead a brand new church plant in a deprived area. He is refining and using my bro-kenness for His glory.

Hannah, UK

I was an angry girl with a whole lot of worldly baggage and weight stacked on my shoulders. I had a yearning for a sort of love that went deeper than anything my parents could give me, despite how amazing they are, or any sort of love a boyfriend or friend could provide. My heart still ached for more.

A particular memory I have is of one day sitting in my room with the sound of my parents arguing, knowing the end of their damaged marriage was impending, and feeling so empty and grey. During such turmoil I came to know Jesus.

There is a sturdiness in my soul that wasn't there before. An anchor, an 'everything's going to be alright' feeling. I didn't have that before. I felt the anger lift from my shoulders that I was carrying around. My outlook on life has completely changed as I fix my eyes on Him. My friends even said since I've been to church I'm so much nicer. I laughed, but it couldn't be more true.

Jessica, UK

What are some key moments in your life that have led you to fall in love with Jesus?

My family never had much growing up so I would say all the time He literally provided for us more than we would need. I specifically remember the time when someone anonymously posted £4000 through our door and kindness like that can't just be a coincidence. It had to be God. To this day we have no idea who it was but we know God did it all!! I also had a similar experience a few years later when I couldn't afford a nice prom dress and someone just gave me the money - NO CLUE WHO!!!! Jesus has always made sure my family and I had more than enough and HOW COULD I NOT LOVE HIM?!

Seeing the love my Mum had for Jesus.

After years of suffering with PTSD, chronic pain and chronic fatigue, just knowing that Jesus was for me and not against me and knowing His presence in my heart was a real turning point. No matter what I'd been through or what I had said or done to him, myself or someone else, He would forgive me and He would still love me unconditionally. That's how amazing the Father's love is.

I feel like Jesus is continually astounding me with his plans and works in my life.

The time when my friend and I were having a conversation about Jesus and we immediately felt the presence of God rest upon us and we just cried our eyes out at the wonder of God.

Invitation to church, meeting great people, the gentleness, grace and kindness of Jesus.

Grandmothers stories.

Multiple people

What are some key moments in your life that have led you to fall in love with Jesus?

In finding a relationship with Him, noticing His goodness in the seemingly small and mundane moments, looking back at past situations and seeing how He has always been faithful to me.

Hearing about the sacrifice He made for me, and everything He gave at the cross, gave me a broader perspective of his grace; getting to worship Him in that made me fall in love with Him even more. Knowing that he's stuck by my side entirely through times when I didn't trust Him, doubted Him or turned to the wrong things when I was hurting, fills me with so much gratitude and makes me cling to His love all the more. When He meets me in the quiet or the low places, I get a full view of His desire to meet me and know me - which is the greatest joy of a relationship with Him.

He healed my dad from Hepatitis C in 2012. I didn't really believe God cared or that prayer worked, but my church prayed consistently, passionately and my dad received treatment that worked for him even though it only had a 10% success rate at that time!! He was healed completely.

I was deaf and when I was 8 I went with my parents to church and got prayed for and suddenly I could hear.

Simple things from him giving me a Bible verse to help calm my fears and big things like mental health restoration & his peace.

Seeing others faithfully living out their lives with purpose and hope.

You know, God's plan is always the best.

Multiple people

I was born and raised in a Christian family, but my family was broken because there was always arguing and tension in my household. Jesus had to become really real to me. He showed me that He wants to use that for good by teaching me from my parents' example what I don't want my life to look like. God did as He promised and miraculously moved 17-year-old me to the city of Baltimore, MD where I attended my senior year of High School and four years of Bible College, graduating with my Bachelor's. During those years God completely shifted things around in me and I was a changed person.

My life is no longer about me but how God can use me and where He wants to direct me. Seeing the importance and urgency of how much people need Christ, I am now serving in my church as we church plant and try to reach those who are unsaved.

Hanna, Hungary

When I was a young child, I saw something I was not supposed to see. When I saw it, my small little mind could not contain it and did not know how to deal with it. Not long after that I fell into an addiction, it wasn't exactly porn but lust, and in my late teens I found out that my addiction was masturbation. I have always been a church girl my entire life. I served, sang at church, and went to church almost every day. But I felt nothing. It felt like I was going to church just because I was obeying my parents. However, In the midst of all that, behind the mask of religion, I was addicted to lust and didn't even know it was a sin - I just knew it felt good, although a little part of me also felt guilty.

Long story short, I went to a youth camp where I was forced to go by my parents. I refused because I was scared of God, and I was comfortable hiding my sin. I knew that something significant was going to happen. It felt like I was going to get exposed, hence my fear. I was afraid people were going to find out that "this faithful Christian girl has been sinning all this time." The Holy Spirit full of kindness encouraged me to go, so I did.

During the camp, someone prayed for me saying, "God misses you so much" and bam, I was crying like a baby and couldn't stop crying for days. I felt His tender love, His heart as a father, and without anyone telling me, I knew He wanted a relationship with me. The one-on-one, the seeking Him in my room with the doors locked, the daily conversations with Him and not just the routine of going to church every week. All of a sudden Jesus felt so close and so loving. That day I accepted Him as my Father. After the encounter, my battles still continued, but Jesus was patient with me.

Jessy, Indonesia

I felt the Holy Spirit telling me to confess the addiction that I was stuck in for eight years. The Holy Spirit reminded me of the verse: "confess your sins and you will be healed." I felt His call into vulnerability, confession and to come out of hiding.

However, confessing was not easy, it was costly; I felt the fear of rejection and a bad reputation but I knew there was nothing to lose, in fact, I was going to gain something greater than what I was going to let go.

I was full of faith and followed my father's lead. He told me to confess to my mom (someone I feared), so I did. What I thought would be my mom's response, God turned around into love and kindness. Instead of being judgemental and angry, my mom cried and hugged me. The pain and burden was lifted at that very moment, I felt light and free. I am happy to say that from that moment till now, God healed me of my addiction.

Jessy, Indonesia

I was broken when Jesus came to save me ten years ago! And for ten years I have been learning every day to live in His grace! You are never too far from God because God is always close to you. His mercy is for everyone.

Alice, France

I had anxiety from a very young age. That developed into Anorexia when I was 13 and social pressures at school didn't help at all. I had to attend appointments each week and gain weight, this was the start of an extremely turbulent five years. I became extremely violent and more and more ill.

I attacked my parents and young sisters and destroyed my home to the point my parents had to call the police. I had anxiety attacks and no social life. Instead I starved myself and did copious amounts of exercise all day just to cope with the noise in my mind.

I was admitted to an inpatient unit. I remember that day so clearly. I didn't talk to any of my family for the whole day. I told them how much I hated them. I got to my tiny room, with a bed, wooden desk and hospital features. As I watched my parents walk away from the hospital, leaving me there, I started sobbing at the window and cried out, "Mumma come back, please." My parents were both standing in the distance crying and waving at me. It was a horrible place, so clinical and lonely. Life revolved around set meals and physical checks and doctors. But their God was so good to me, I know He was with me even if I didn't realise it at the time. I was discharged, then COVID happened and I relapsed very, very badly. I started running away from home, starving myself to try and numb the intense emotions in my head. Again. I went to an emergency appointment. The nurse looked at me and said I had to go to A and E because my blood pressure and weight was dangerously low.

I ran away from home but I was finally admitted to a paediatric ward. I refused to eat any food or drink . My brain was so starved that I was diagnosed with Psychosis. I didn't recognise

Emma, UK

my mum, I would attack those around me, I would try and kill myself. All I would do is pace up and down and repeat the phrase, 'mummy I'm overwhelmed, I can't cope'. My mum had to do everything for me: wash me, stop me from banging my head against walls, and comfort me in my extreme distress. It got to the point where they had to force-feed me using a tube. It was the most horrible experience of my life. I was restrained by lots of strangers on a hospital table.

But as I stared in that moment, I remember God speaking to me so clearly, saying, "you don't need to fight this battle anymore, I'm fighting it for you". That evening I broke down. I asked Jesus to bear all of my burdens because I literally had no strength left in me. I felt this unbelievable peace wash over me. Comfort I had never ever felt during my five years of illness.

The next morning, breakfast came and I usually would never eat it but this time I cried out to Him and I ate everything. He put this verse in my head: 'trust in the Lord with all your heart and lean not on your own understanding, in all your ways acknowledge him and he will direct your paths'. The same thing happened over the course of the time that I was there.

I wrote a diary throughout my whole time and you can literally see Jesus in my thoughts! I was discharged and sent to the inpatient unit again which was very tough. I didn't know who I was anymore. But slowly Jesus taught me my identity is in Him alone.

I've been out of the hospital and all mental health services since. The doctors at my discharge meeting were amazed! They said "we've never seen a patient like you with the hope you have"

Emma, UK

and I started crying because that's when it hit me that Jesus was the only person who healed me. He was my hope and He still is my friend and comforter.

I still find things hard, and my mind still afflicts me, but I cope differently. I have a Saviour who is in the boat with me, during the storm. I have Jesus who I can trust and be real with. He has set me free on His cross and ultimately that's all I need to rejoice in!

Emma, UK

My life was full of family who loved Jesus, so I always had an understanding of who He was from a distant place. But, when I met Him for myself I realised life before felt fairly empty!!! I didn't have a strong identity or understand who I really was and who He was to me.

Encountering Him has been everything. I have had too many encounters to ever doubt how good and how kind He is; His presence is tangible and He is close like a Father! When I gave my life to Jesus I will never forget the feeling of a warm shower all over my body from head to toe, I felt the safety and the embrace of who I know now as a loving, safe and perfect Father who chose me before I chose Him!!

Since then I have continued to encounter Him in tangible ways. I experience His presence and His closeness in physical and emotional ways and in my thought patterns. He is the best and is kind in being near to me in my pain and my brokenness and I have experienced His unconditional love as I have let Him into the most vulnerable places of my heart!

Jon, UK

Looking back, I think I was quite a gossipy person and had some very difficult friendships. I don't think I was very nice to be around. This was mostly in school during Year 7 and Year 8, which is quite a difficult time for everyone anyway, what with figuring out secondary school and the year completely revolving around who was in the 'popular' group! I guess that quickly became my priority and I definitely wasn't always kind or self-less to those around me.

I felt like being from a Christian family was weird and uncool with my new friends, so although I still went to church with my family, I dropped away from my youth group. I didn't pray or spend time with God and had a lot of doubts about God and Christianity being real.

My closest friends who knew me then joke that those were my 'Dark Lizzy' days, which thankfully is proof, I guess, that I'm a different person now. I remember going to a Christian festival with my family. Everyone around me was worshipping and talking about God and how amazing faith is; I wanted to believe but I just couldn't convince myself. So I decided to go for prayer for my lack of faith. The person praying for me simply asked God to show me a sign that He was real. Her boldness shocked me. It randomly popped into my head that I wanted a certain person I literally never spoke to, to text me, as a sign, and I remember making this 'deal' with God in my head. If it happened, it would show me He was there. And two hours later, I got back to our accommodation and there was a random message from them! I remember crying and being in awe that God could use something as trivial as Snapchat to speak to me.

After this, I decided to start reading the Bible again and pray

Lizzy, UK

more. I became good friends with someone at school who was really struggling with their mental health, and I remember having no idea how to help. As well as just being there to listen to them, I started to share a little bit of my faith (however tentative it was) and how I believed Jesus loved them, had a purpose for their life. My friend showed interest so I invited them to my youth group. They accepted, and that meant I actually had to go too, for the first time in a long time!

From then on my own relationship with God and boldness in sharing faith has grown massively, as I was stuck back into a loving Christian community and actively seeking closeness with Jesus. I started to see prayers answered in both my own and my friend's life, which strengthened my faith even more. He is worthy to be praised and doesn't let me down.

My perspective and opinions on the world changed from worldly to Godly. When I broke up with my boyfriend I was lost and I knew I needed something to fill me and make me feel wanted, I found that in God.

I attended a conference held in the O2 arena that my friend had invited me to. I really only agreed to go because I was bored. Towards the end, the worship leader started singing "Majesty." I had heard the song numerous times before as I grew up in the church. But that day, when they started singing the chorus, "Your grace has found me just as I am", I felt this strong pull and inside me I could hear the voice of God call my name. In a moment, I felt loved and desired like never before.

In a moment, I gave in to that pull and said yes to Jesus. My life changed 180 degrees from that moment. I went home and just sat and read my Bible for hours and hours on end. People that saw me after that said I had a glow on my face. I was so in love with Jesus. I have been ever since that moment. The road has not been easy but Jesus has been so faithful and good to me. He is worthy of everything.

Rachel, UK

I was an atheist and I had insomnia; I couldn't even sleep for longer than half an hour. I had nightmares. I couldn't control my anger, depression and anxiety. I tried to kill myself. Since having Jesus in my life I've had no insomnia, no depression, no anxiety and I can control my anger. I also was addicted to cigarettes and weed but Jesus has helped me to stop doing that. He's always with me and never lets me down.

Shayan, Iran

I would say that I've always known Jesus, or at least I've known about him. I grew up in a Christian family, so at Sunday school I was taught how to pray, and we would read Bible stories. When I was about 12, I first properly encountered Him - it wasn't this crazy moment of revelation but it was this deep sense of knowing that I'm so truly and completely loved and I let Him into my life.

I'm sure lots of people have struggled with this but at this point, I also struggled with porn. I've never properly talked about it because I've always been ashamed of it, but I can remember the first time I voiced it to someone at my church youth group and they didn't judge me, they didn't think any less of me; they hugged me and prayed for me and all I felt in that moment was Jesus.

Jessica, UK

I grew up in a Christian household so I was always hearing about Him, going to church every Sunday and learning about Him but I didn't really have a 'relationship' with Him. At a festival, I decided I wanted God at the very centre of my life. School for me has become a huge challenge as being a Christian isn't easy and girls can be brutal, but knowing that I can put my problems in God's hands has pulled me through.

I lost my confidence in Year 9, I started to feel anxious all the time and I would get stomach aches whenever I felt nervous. I still struggle with it but knowing my Creator and friend is with me every step has helped me so much. I've tried to seek approval from many things but I've found that now it's only God whom I seek approval from. I love Jesus, He is my best friend and I am so proud to be a part of God's family.

Marli, UK

It always felt like God was chasing me down. When going through a tough time of bullying at high school I turned to the Bible and the words were so comforting! I prayed even though I'd never been taught how, it just felt so natural and on days when I was fully expecting to get attacked, He protected me.

I once got invited to a youth group, was prayed for and was filled with the Holy Spirit. Wow! I felt the Lord's warmth and power. Worship music captivated me and helped me on my journey. I was learning to play the drums throughout high school and when I heard modern Christian music with real drums in it I was hooked! Jesus used that to bring me closer and give me the heart to serve in worship.

Throughout my late teens my life changed, Jesus built up my confidence and helped me become a worshipper and follower. Now, aged 29, I have an amazing wife, a tech job and I get to lead my church family in worship. I've had moments where I fell away but life always got so lonely and meaningless and complicated and dark without Him. Thank you, Jesus!

Jamie, UK

I feel so blessed to have grown up in a Christian home, and I gave my life to Christ when I was a young child but I've really got to know Him more in the last year. I used to be timid in my faith, afraid to pray for people, afraid to speak about Jesus. I was trying to be a good enough person so Jesus could use me but now I know Jesus died to free me from the trap of comparison and fear and can use me as broken as I may be!

I used to think Christianity was old-fashioned and outdated but now I love Jesus and know I couldn't do life without Him! Jesus is my comfort in suffering, my best friend in loneliness, and my guide for my future. I lean on Him. My life would look totally different if Jesus wasn't a part of it.

Naomi, UK

Peace is my biggest promise, I go through a lot of highs and lows and God has been constant, ever faithful, present, and actively engaging in my day-to-day life. From the smallest to the biggest things in my life.

I grew up in a Christian home but never had a personal relationship with God. Church was a very boring chore once a week, and the Bible was just a restrictive rule book! When I got older, I was depressed and looked for joy and satisfaction in the world. I started drinking a lot with my friends and I had a boyfriend. We set no boundaries and did whatever we wanted. But I was still depressed! I kept trying but nothing bought me lasting joy.

One day in lockdown, I met a stranger on a beach. We started chatting and straight away I realised there was something different, something special about him. He declined the offer of a beer, same with a cigarette. He only spoke highly of others and spoke with such joy and a massive smile across his face. I soon realised that what made him special is that he loved Jesus. He shone His love and light, and it was clear to see the Spirit lived in him.

I then realised that I had to make a choice. I can continue living this life of constantly searching for joy, or I can surrender my all to the true, and only source of lasting joy and satisfaction: Jesus! We walked together from there on, keeping each other accountable, encouraging each other and sharing what it really means to be a follower of Christ. I stopped getting drunk, broke up with my boyfriend, and pursued purity, and I now just love reading the bible! It is not a book of rules and restrictions but of freedom and fatherly love and care. I can't wait to serve Jesus all of my life!!

Jess, UK

How has life changed since having Jesus in your life?

I found hope.

I have experienced so much peace in busy and uncertain seasons, such as exams, university entrance and family illness. I honestly don't know how I would live without knowing that there is a God out there who loves me.

I am so much more confident in who I was created to be! I used to be so insecure in myself but now I know that I am beautiful.

Every day I wake up knowing I am already loved, already enough, already seen! Everything else is just an extra! Knowing Jesus and the Father has radically changed my life and helped me become who I am today. It has also helped me understand who I am called to be and my purpose here on earth!

Life isn't always easy as a Christian, but knowing that Jesus loves me unconditionally and that He will never leave me makes difficult situations easier to cope/live with/through.

An ultimate peace knowing that I am not alone and not in control.

Not suicidal, not depressed and not abusing alcohol.

There is not a day that goes by that I question my worth and the love Jesus has for me. In a world where everything is so uncertain and scary, I cling on to the fact I am a daughter of Jesus. Every day is a joyful one no matter what.

I used to have bad anxiety and depression, but now I find peace and comfort in Christ.

Multiple people

How has life changed since having Jesus in your life?

Everything has changed for the better. Jesus has become my comfort and joy in everything. It's like having a best friend, parent and family all in one. I'm slowly learning to love myself, love the people around me and love Him more and more.

I truly believe that He has helped with my struggles, with my anxiety and my mental health, which have significantly improved since I decided to trust in Jesus.

Whoever I am, whatever I choose to be, whatever mistakes I make, I know that I'm loved with unfailing love I feel free, loved, held, comforted, supported and finally have started to like myself, just as He wants me to.

I have freedom and peace like no other.

I have a purpose, significance and a secure identity.

I have become more devoted to spending time with God. I have become more humble, and patient and even tried talking less and listening more. I feel refreshed and loved.

It has definitely done a full 180 and I am finally living freely and I have so much Joy and Hope.

I know where I can place my identity and where I can find joy, because it's a source that never changes, never runs dry and never disappoints! I have a Heavenly Father who delights in seeing me grow, and I love dedicating my life and plans to Him.

It's changed everything. From hopelessness to an overflowing hope for life.

Multiple people

Anorexia had consumed my life and I didn't even know at this point it was an illness. I hated myself so much and I thought God hated me. Doctors were working with me as an outpatient at the young people's department for Mental Health Disorders, but they wanted to admit me into the hospital full-time. They didn't trust me living at home as I was losing weight rapidly.

Fast forward to a Christian event I was attending - I remember feeling something pull me to go to the front for prayer. This was so out of character of me at this point because I didn't think God would ever want me. I now know that this pull was the Holy Spirit. A pastor prayed for me and I suddenly felt a huge washing of God's presence which all I can describe as a weighty love that just washed over me, and it kept coming.

It was the best feeling I had ever felt and I knew it was God. I kept crying, like a really good, deep cry. And I knew it was His love. I heard His voice for the first time and He said, "I see you and I love you, I know everything about you and I still love you!". Something broke in me and I felt and knew I was His daughter. He wanted me and loved me, even in my darkest moments. In this encounter with God, I felt Him break off the eating disorder from my identity.

I still had Anorexia but I knew I was worth the fight and this was not part of my identity. I went on a journey of healing the next year and that was a defining encounter for me as I became a Child of God and knew my identity as His daughter and His love for me. In less than a year I was discharged from the Mental Health Hospital and I was free from Anorexia. I had a relationship with Jesus. Twelve years later, after that encounter, I am even more in love with Jesus than ever before.

Rebekah, UK

He has continued to heal me, I didn't have my periods for 5 years and He has restored them and now I have a beautiful daughter and an amazing husband. My life has continually changed. I felt my world went from black and white to colour. Don't get me wrong, there have been hard times since then but I have never felt alone and I can honestly say that my life changed so dramatically as Jesus was the one I was searching for my whole life. Jesus has given me peace which is something so precious to me. He has given me and continues to give me joy that goes beyond circumstances. He has given me a love that makes me at home in myself.

Rebekah, UK

I always believed God was there, I just didn't think He liked me very much! I didn't pursue a relationship with God until I was 16, so life before then felt like I was always chasing after something, never feeling fulfilled or purposeful.

I would compare myself to everyone around me, especially girls, and never feel good enough. I was so insecure and unhappy with myself, I didn't see myself as precious or worth much. I tried to find validation in what others thought of me and if I was seen as pretty and skinny by boys. It was hard!

I was still battling with insecurities and comparison when God spoke to me through three different people, all of whom had the word 'precious' for me. My name is Gemma and in the bible, it means 'precious', so this word has always been special to me. I sobbed each time God spoke the word 'precious' over me through those people and felt the Holy Spirit! I knew God was speaking to me and I had to listen.

The fact that God made it so obvious to me that I am His precious daughter whom He dearly loves, just made me fall in love with Him. God just showed me that I am unique and precious, and soooo worth dying for! I now feel confident and happy in my own skin, it took years for that to happen but God made it happen. I have a beautiful church community, a kingdom purpose, and unending love from King Jesus. Jesus is Life.

Gemma, UK

When I started secondary school I denied Jesus for a year because I was too scared of what other people would think of me being a Christian. I broke down and repented at a church camp. I just felt Jesus's loving arms of forgiveness wrap around me. I've tried to be brave and bold in my faith ever since. However, I am still learning.

Joy is tattooed on my ankle because that is what my life is now full of! Joy in everything. The ups, the downs, the exciting events and the stressful ones. Joy is woven into every part.

Erin, UK

When everything was falling apart, I felt God embrace me. I felt seen and loved. He is faithful.

I grew up in a home where Jesus was very much present, and I haven't had many moments where I've felt like I turned my back on Him completely (which I am hugely grateful for). But I had a period in my life where it very much felt like I wanted to walk away.

For a while, when I listened for God's voice or sat with Him in prayer, the first thing I would always hear was, "I love you". And to hear that from the person that knows every part of me and the thought that runs through my head is mind-blowing. The weight of the things I've done and said falls off and I know everything I deal with I can take to Him. He knows exactly how I'm feeling and how to minister to me if I ask. Life feels colourful again. He knows what's best for me. He led me into a job that I didn't think I'd love, but have grown to absolutely invest my heart and soul into.

Kate, UK

I'm a pastor's kid, so I've always been around the church. When I turned 12 I decided that I didn't want to be a Christian because I found it boring and there were always people putting loads of expectations on me just because I was the Pastor's kid. My only focus was on my swimming training and making friends to become more "popular".

I started volunteering at church on a Saturday just because I wanted to "please" my parents, because even though I was angry at them I never wanted them to feel bad. Turns out I started to enjoy being at church and helping on a team which meant I missed out on a lot of hangouts with my non-Church friends. After a few weeks, I lost all of my friends because they tagged me as a "Christian".

One day, I turned on my computer and saw a text from my dad. He sent me a link to a pastor preaching, I played the video and the words he said were literally a word from God to me.

He said:
"Move now,
From dead to life,
From bondage to freedom,
From mourning to dancing,
From defeat to victory,
From shame to grace,
From fear to faith,
Move now…
We're not waiting on the move of God, we are the move of God, so move now!".

That morning I decided to move, I gave my life to Jesus and He

Aaron, Mexico

healed my heart, my anger was gone, my frustration was gone, and it was replaced with a passion for young people; for my friends. Since then I've been moving and chasing after God's call for my life. Every day I pray, "God I want to see what you can do through me", and He's done some pretty cool stuff: first in me, then through me.

The first time God spoke to me was when I was three years old. I remember that He filled me with His love and joy when I was six. His awesomeness was revealed during worship when I was nine. The time He tore fear out of me as I lay on the floor unable to get up when I was ten. His realness was apparent throughout my teenage years. The friend He became when I was nineteen (I'd always thought of Him as a Father or Brother - most of my friends had moved away, openly rejected me, or died up to that point, so a Friend who never left was overwhelming to me.) When I started stepping out into the workplace after college, He went with me as my biggest encourager and mentor. Oh my, God is Awesome!!!

I grew up in a Christian household so I always knew God, but I did not have a personal relationship with Him. I gave my life to Christ when I was 8 years old and rededicated my life when I was 14.

I had some trouble at college and university and I developed anxiety and depression. I had to transfer back home from university and I just felt like a failure and thought, 'why would God let this happen to me?'. I began to resent Him and didn't really want anything to do with Him, however the only thing that seemed to give me a sense of peace was worship music and I would play it every night to go to sleep.

My parents started at Bible college at this point and I found it so strange, I hated it and thought I would never ever ever do something like that. I remember one night I was lying in bed crying out to God, asking Him to show Himself to me because I needed to feel something. A few days later I went to a bible study about speaking in tongues where I was filled with the Holy Spirit. Someone gave me a word, which was exactly what I'd been praying to God about that night - I thought, 'that's strange… how do they know what I was saying to God?'. Some days later my bestie and I were talking and again she said something which is exactly what I'd been praying to God about.

Fast forward a few months and I'd joined Bible college and completed it, not without struggles and pain, but I came out of it and wow, God was so so evident and tangible in those last few months. He is so good, His plan is perfect and I've learnt that all I need to do is surrender my life to Him. He is always there and He always shows up, it's just a matter of seeing that and noticing it.

Bek, UK

I grew up in a Christian household, part of a small church community that my parents ran. I didn't have many friends at church and Christian summer camps basically sustained my faith. At the age of 17, I decided to leave my faith behind and come back to it when I wanted to settle down. The following week my Dad, (who had no idea about the conclusion I had come to) preached on 2 Peter 2:21 and it struck me in my heart and I realised I shouldn't give up on faith.

Whilst at uni, I struggled to navigate a good balance of partying, uni and faith until someone spoke to me about leading something and I felt the responsibility not to be a hypocritical leader, but rather one filled with integrity.

I then came to a church and went away with the Youth as a team member and was so impacted by their freedom and joy that I decided to move to work for the church to follow a sense of call to help young people.

Jesus has completely changed my life. My whole life's purpose has become dedicated to sharing Jesus and His grace, freedom and love. I never expected my life to look like this, (I expected to work in marketing in London) but I wouldn't change it for the world.

Lizzie, UK

I started trying to fit in and be best friends with a group of people who were a bad influence on me. I started chasing worldly things and I became depressed and struggled mentally more than I ever have in my life. I ended up getting into a relationship with a boy who was just using me. I was lying to my parents about who I was with and what I was doing that regularly. I started to self-harm and I was so down all the time, I eventually became suicidal.

Throughout all of this I never once talked to anyone because I didn't want to be a burden. I didn't want my parents to know because they had already gone through stuff like this with my older brother. I saw how much it had hurt them - so I kept it all to myself, which made it worse and made me feel so much more alone. Eventually, the boy realised he couldn't use me anymore and ended things with me, which I was so grateful for as I felt like I couldn't end it, even though I wanted to.

God brought a really special person into my life who spoke to me about God's heart for me. The end of that relationship actually improved my mental health quite a bit, as I had been trying to gain worth from my boyfriend - which was empty and never fulfilling.

I have not been suicidal since, I have not self-harmed since, and I am pursuing a relationship with God, and my life is so much more fulfilling. Thank you, Jesus.

Emma, New Zealand

I didn't grow up in church or around people who loved Jesus, however, I always believed that there was this 'man in the sky' who takes care of people. In 2018 my mum was diagnosed with Breast Cancer and that's when I decided there was no God. The loving God everyone talks about is not for me. He doesn't love our family, instead He punished us, so why would I believe in Him?

My mum never knew Jesus and denied Him all her life until a year before she passed away. It was just a couple of months before Covid where she fell in love with Him. During Covid, she attended an online church and I wasn't interested. I was so depressed, there wouldn't be a night without tears, nightmares and suicidal thoughts during the period when she was ill. I was a totally different person.

However, at that time I didn't think Jesus was for me. I blamed God for everything that has happened. Until the day she passed away, when I encountered Jesus' love for the first time. I was grieving, and still am, but I was surrounded by His love. It's hard to explain, it was a feeling I had never experienced. I started reading the Bible, praying, and listening to worship songs and slowly I started falling in love with Jesus..

My friend encouraged me to find a local church that I could attend regularly, but I was a bit hesitant as I thought I could do this without a community: I can read the Bible at home by myself, I can pray by myself, I can listen to worship at home, why would I need people? This was my mindset until one day when I found a church and I decided to go, and I was welcomed into their family from day one. Jesus showed up every time ever since! And I don't think I would've grown in my relationship

Daniela, Romania

with Jesus on my own.

I went on a young adults retreat with a group from church and that's when I felt Jesus on a different level! The amount of love I felt at that moment cannot be described. A few months after, my love for Jesus grew even stronger and I decided to get baptised. Praise the Lord! The best decision ever!

Life before Christ was:
W- worries
E- exhaustion
I- indecisive
R- rocky
D- depression

From WEIRD to BLESSED

B- bloom
L- loving
E- enjoyable
S- saved
S- safe
E- exciting
D- determined

Daniela, Romania

I've been through things from a pretty young age that I'm certain I wouldn't have gotten through without God's supernatural hope. His Spirit dwelling within me provides courage and strength for each day. Looking back on those times now, like when I was 15, taking important exams and both my parents were seriously ill and undergoing chemo/radiotherapy. Being able to see God's faithfulness to bring me through a time I didn't know how to live through, makes me love Him even more. Seeing in my own life that He is so devoted to me, He is able and He has always been there even when I don't see it.

Anonymous

I've known Jesus since I was a child through a Christian up-bringing, but I feel that I 'met' Jesus properly and for myself when I was 15 years old. Life and teenage years before that were a mixture of loss, hurt and shame. I didn't know who I was or what my purpose was. Self-hatred consumed me. I was lost in a closed-off world that no one seemed to enter - Until Jesus did. It seemed all I wanted to do was hate Jesus. However, He brought me in even closer. He loved me and still loves me with an un-shakable force and dragged me from the sadness and self-hatred that seemed to follow me wherever I went.

I grew up in a Christian home, with God-loving parents and grandparents. You could say I have had it so easy and in many ways I have, (and I definitely count myself so blessed in that), but equally, my journey to discover for myself who Jesus is, has been long and bumpy. It has taken me much of my life to really understand who He is and I'm still learning every day.

I know that my grandparents had a profound impact on my life and my trajectory, as they prayed for me daily when they were alive, which I am so thankful for.

Prayers are never wasted. I made the choice to follow Jesus a few times when growing up, often at 'Christian events' where there was an altar call or a 'prayer' said. The first time I prayed this I was 8 years old. I think each time I prayed it, I wanted to be absolutely sure I had done it right and I worried that the previous time I did it wasn't enough. It has taken me quite a few years to understand that God doesn't want our perfection, He just wants our heart, and each day that I step further into this truth, I find greater depths of freedom and hope, that leave me speechless enough to just want to worship Him with all I have.

As I grow with age and experience, I find myself more and more dependent on Him each day and asking for the Holy Spirit to give me grace, wisdom and strength to make it through the day. He is so gracious and kind, and I honestly don't know how people do life without Jesus!

Christelle, UK

I had always been surrounded by faith. When I was 10 I attended a Christian festival where I gave my life to Jesus. A few years on, my curiosity began to grow and I started to question my beliefs, my heart began to harden and I started doing things and watching things that I knew were wrong.

Each time my conscience told me what I was doing was wrong and I would then feel shameful and unworthy - this changed when I was 13 and slowly God began to soften my heart and the struggles I once walked in began to fall off.

I realised the true meaning of Jesus' death on the Cross. I began to think about how in the Old Testament, humans presented animals as sacrifices for their sins and how in the New Testament, God sent His son, Jesus as a sacrifice for my sins, meaning I no longer have to strive to make it up to God because Jesus' blood covers it all!

The Lord is patiently and compassionately teaching me about the freedom Christ's death means for me. He's breaking the chains that religion had on my life and revealing the bright and colourful future He has in store for my life!

Lydia, UK

What has helped you most in your walk with Jesus?

Reading the Bible has been a massive help, and most important-
ly, seeking the Lord when reading it. Using podcasts, books, and
devotionals to understand what it teaches us about God and see
the context and intention of the passage. I believe the Bible is
the living Word of God, and that it has the power to sustain us
spiritually and it's important to read it as a daily habit. I've found
that hard to do as I'm not much of a reader, but Jesus just wants
our heart and our devotion, not our perfection, so don't be too
hard on yourself! Ask Jesus to give you such a passion and
desire for His Word so that you can't go a day without it, as
Jesus delights in moulding our hearts to become more like His,
and He is continually moulding me.

Community.

Worship music.

Knowing Him as my Father. I never knew my biological father,
and my life was overwhelmed with abandonment and rejection.

People who surround me and uplift me. People who pray for me,
worship with me and read the bible with me.

Accountability, wise counsel and great friends.

Without a doubt, my bible and my friendships.

His presence, His comfort and His love.

Learning to be alone with Him and the importance of the secret
place. Being with Him each day is the most important thing we
can do.

Multiple people

What has helped you most in your walk with Jesus?

I've journaled a TON! Writing has helped me process things, it's allowed me to slow down, and let my brain catch up a bit and has allowed Jesus to speak to me in many ways. Having close friends who have been there when I've fallen apart, been vulnerable with me, lifted me up and have prayed for me has been a huge blessing.

Worship, I come home from school sometimes feeling emotionally drained and I put on some worship music and it just helps so much.

Staying close to Him, Abiding well with Him, Dependency , intimacy daily, Prayer, Lots of prayer, Worship as warfare, Taking Him at His word and Not entertaining the enemy's lies. Being known and knowing Him.

Friends - accountability!! Being friends with people who are also striving towards wholeness in Christ, seeing them as good examples and encouraging each other. Listening to the right voices!

Talking to Him. There have been times when I've enjoyed the daily morning routine of reading my bible and writing things down and there have also been times, especially since becoming a parent, when that's been almost non-existent. But just taking moments throughout the day when I'm in the car, when I open my eyes in the morning for 30 seconds, while my son naps or I'm eating lunch, just to say hi and chat to Him about what's going on. To listen to what He wants to tell me, and asking for His help when I need his wisdom. Just involving him in my day-to-day, and allowing Him to be my friend. Letting Him show me how to be more like Him.

Multiple people

Life was okay. I have grown up in a non-Christian family all my life. A friend brought me along to a youth group about 4 years ago. I mainly went because it meant I could hang out with my friends and have a lot of fun!!

I went to a Christian camp and I met Jesus! I was going through school and I wasn't very confident in myself. I used to be so insecure in myself but now I know that I am a beautiful creation! I am able to have so much more joy and hope in every circumstance and I know that Jesus has an amazing plan for my life.

Eliza, UK

I live knowing I'm safe, watched over, and championed, meaning I can take each day with confidence about my inward and outward view on my life and how I can influence others. I feel brighter each day, I'm working on my relationship with God, who is His children's biggest fan!

Beth, UK

I came to know Jesus at a festival when I was 17. I'd been an atheist since deciding at age 10 that I didn't understand church or God and didn't want anything to do with Him any longer. My friend persuaded me to go to this festival promising that, 'It wouldn't really be that Christian' and that we could just 'say a quick prayer in the morning and then we can have fun'. I begrudgingly went. As soon as we went into the worship I felt this strange fire in my heart. We started singing, 'consuming fire, fan into flame' and I was so surprised to find that this fire we were singing about was in my heart.

I discovered that God existed and He loved me. I went back to my tent that evening feeling that God was with me in it. I said to Him, 'How can you be here? I thought if You existed, You'd be up there in the sky, but You're here with me in my tent'.

A few months later when I was back home, I started to doubt what had happened and put it down to my imagination. But later that day, I opened my bible and discovered Luke 24:32. The verse said, 'Were not our hearts burning within us while He talked with us on the road?' From then on I believed, as I realised this same experience I'd had, had also been experienced by the disciples 2000 years ago. It convinced me that it all must be true.

Anonymous

Everything has changed for the better. Jesus has become my comfort and joy in everything. It's like having a best friend, parent and family all in one. I'm slowly learning to love myself, love the people around me and love Him more and more.

I was bullied really badly in school. It started when I was 11. I had acne, I was tall, I was the only English girl with a funny name (Beth, not very Spanish!), and everything in my life was falling apart. I spent every break time and lunch break in the bathrooms in school, eating my snack/lunch by myself. The church my family and I were a part of fell apart, I didn't have any friends and pushed my family away. I was completely and utterly alone. I would cry myself to sleep every night begging, and I mean begging through sobs, that God would take me in my sleep… That I wouldn't ever wake up. I wished for that for about a year. But a year passed and I was still waking up in the morning, so I remember telling God that if He didn't kill me by the end of the week, I'd do it myself.

On a Thursday, my mum came into my room and asked me how I would feel about moving back to the UK, just for a year to be close to my family. That was my way out of everything. So I said to God, "Fine, I'll live and we'll move away. But if I get bullied in my new school, or if I don't make any friends then I'm done". He saved my life. I went to a little Christian school where I met the most wonderful girls ever and we're still best friends now. That year was really tough though, I experienced grief for the first time, and I fell in love for the first time but through all of that God put people around me to help shape me and help me grow. I got baptised that year and fully rejoiced in knowing who God was to me, not to my parents, or my church, but to me.

We moved back to Spain after that year, but to a different city, so I went to a different school and made new friends. When I moved away from home I fell into a pool of loneliness. My first time away from home, I was working long hours to raise money

Beth, Spain

for upcoming mission trips. I couldn't go to church because I worked Sundays too. I stopped eating, people had made comments about my weight all my life, and without my parents around to keep tabs on me, I just gave up. I didn't eat, not properly for about 4 months.

I came back to Spain for the holidays and my mum noticed how much weight I'd lost but didn't ask anything further. It was during my trip to Guinea Bissau when I fainted because I was so weak, and I realised I had a problem. I was diagnosed with Anorexia. It was a tricky recovery to make, but that's when I grew and found God properly for the first time by myself without my parents and that's when my faith became my own. I understood that I was made in His image, and that I am loved unconditionally.

Through everything that happened to me, He was in control and had been looking over me all those years. I'm doing a lot better now, summer isn't great for someone like me with body dysmorphia but I have a strong foundation in who I am in Christ and I truly believe for the first time in my life that I am loved no matter what. And I am completely and utterly beautiful.

Beth, Spain

3 days after my 9th birthday my dad suffered a brain haemor-
rhage, he was paralysed down the left side and things were not
good. The surgeon had to operate on him again a couple of days
later to relieve the pressure on the brain. He told my mum he
had done all he could and we should go home and pray. So my
mum, my sister and I went home and prayed on our knees. My
prayer was simple: "Jesus, if you save my dad, I will love you
forever." He did.

We then went to church every Sunday. I couldn't get enough of
it. I was a Sunday school teacher at the age of 16, I was the
youngest elder in our district at the age of 24. I was part of the
church dance group, I learnt guitar for church. All was good.
Our minister announced that there was to be a coach going to
Aberdeen for a crusade, mum asked if I wanted to go, I said no!
This went on for 3 weeks, then the last week it was announced
something nudged me to say yes, there were 2 seats left on the
bus, God is good. What an amazing time, thousands of people
worshipping, people crying uncontrollably, but not knowing
why the thousands of people were answering the altar call. It all
stirred my soul and I rededicated my life to the Lord.

Denise, UK

As each day goes past I feel so at peace with His plan for my life, as I see it falling into place. God's plan for my life has been completely different to the plan I had made myself. It has been so humbling watching my own plans crumble and watching God's plans work in wonderful ways which I could never have imagined. It has taught me to trust in Jesus each and every day.

In times when it's impossible to know why God's plan is looking different or scary from that of our own, His plan is good. There is not a day that goes by that I question my worth and the love Jesus has for me. In a world where everything is so uncertain and scary, I cling on to the fact I am a daughter of Jesus. Every day is a joyful one no matter what.

Isabelle, UK

In the summer of 2012, my dad became ill and it was apparent that I was being led to go home again to help with his care. My mom had to become the sole breadwinner for our family and I had a younger sister still in the house so my mom needed help. When I came home, I was shocked of the darkness in my house. The health issues my dad was facing (and how that impacted all of us in the family) made our home environment very toxic. He was angry and bitter. As his health declined, even more, it all culminated in his eventual suicide in 2015. What an immense loss. What a shock. It was the darkness of the pain of loss and suicide loss, that forever changed my life. So much was shattered on that day. Not to mention that leaving my life in Florida, and the friends I cared about the most, was the death of a lot of dreams. It was such a sacrifice and for it only to end up this way? I could hardly believe it.

I couldn't see Jesus in those days at all. I knew He was there of course, but I couldn't feel Him. Just numbness. All I can say is God helped me survive when I thought that may not even be possible. And God was even better than I could have dreamed. I remember after my dad died, God saying, "Someday, you'll look at this as a blessing". Initially, I reeled from the thought of that. How on earth could that ever happen?? But after all this time, I can see how Jesus brought it to pass. My experience has been a blessing for those who I sit with, and who have also experienced suicide loss. Any comfort I can give is because it's the comfort the Father has given to me. I'm watching my life bloom and unfold in ways I never expected. But I am forever grateful that Jesus saw me through.

Maryssa, USA

My mum passed away in 2018 and I inherited our copy of the family tree and a box full of family Bibles, dating back to 1887. Included was our family's Welsh Bible from 1899. You would think with such a rich heritage it would have been an easy step and decision for me to make to become a follower of Jesus.

Unfortunately, I don't know why but for some reason in my early teenage years I developed quite a large chip on my shoulder and matched it with a strong will. I wasn't the most pleasant person to be around as my long-suffering parents and siblings knew all too well. If the truth is known, I didn't like myself very much either.

I remember during those very hard, trying years my Dad saying to me often, 'There is a beautiful girl inside of me just waiting to get out', and one night when I was eighteen, after living my way for far too long, and finally getting sick of myself and how I was living, I cried out to the Lord and He heard me. Everything changed from that moment, I was a new person. The next day my Dad was in the backyard and I went up to him and said, "Dad, you know how you always said there was a beautiful girl inside of me just waiting to get out?". I put out my hand and shook his hand and said, "I'm very pleased to meet you". The best decision of my life. I had a new life.

All things were changed and new relationships that I thought would never recover were beautifully restored. I was born again in the most beautiful way. I have a twin sister and she often says that she became more committed to her faith because of the undeniable change she had seen in me.

Leanne, Australia

Back in 2012, my mom dropped the bomb on me that we would be moving to another city. I was 16, depressed, extremely lonely, self-harming regularly, drinking, making very big mistakes and contemplating taking my own life. Things were very hard, but for some reason, I was reluctant for a new start. My mom is a total hero because I fought her every step of the way, but she knew what was best for me. We eventually moved to our new city, and two days later I started at my new school. It was an all-girls school which absolutely terrified me because I had struggled with a couple of mean girls at my last school (which was one of the big factors in why we moved.)

However, the lovely girl who gave me a tour of my new school was a breath of fresh air. At the end of the tour, she said a bus comes to collect all of us at 6pm on a Friday night and we head through to a youth ministry together. I thought to myself, "it's pretty weird that this entire school goes to a youth ministry to-gether, but I'll give it a go!" Turns out it wasn't compulsory, but I had completely misunderstood the assignment! I went anyway and turned up at youth on a Friday night. It was so different to any other youth ministry I had ever been a part of. It was full of joy and laughter and fun, but I could tell there was a total depth to what was happening. As the night went on, I felt the tangible presence of God for the first time. I heard the word of God come alive for the first time and ended the night giving my heart to Jesus.

From there I thought, man if they are ever looking for youth leaders I would love to be involved (but was convinced they wouldn't want someone as broken as me.) By the end of the year, I decided to be bold and ask the youth pastor if they needed any help with anything, and from there my journey of

Emma, South Africa

serving in the house of God began. At a youth day event, I felt the spirit of God drop in my heart that I must no longer be a spectator in His kingdom and that it was time to participate. I have never looked back!

Jesus completely stopped me in my tracks as a 16-year-old girl and took all of my plans and set them aside. Now, I am a married youth pastor in the same church, and my husband and I have the honour of leading our national youth ministry. I still can't believe it, and it is still the greatest honour of my life to be a host in the house of the Lord! Through my weakness, He was made strong. He healed my heart, wiped my slate clean and gave me a new start. I love Jesus with every fibre of my being!

Emma, South Africa

After our first son was born, we were pregnant again and moved house quickly to a place God had been preparing. I was 7 months pregnant and 2.5 months after moving, our second was full term and ended up being a stillborn little girl. There was no reason why she passed or what had caused it. We accepted this assignment God presented and was full of so much peace and grace through the process but definitely mourned her passing.

During this same time (still not sure why these happened simultaneously), my husband had confessed to infidelity years back that he had kept a secret. He was repentant and wanted to stay married... But dealing with a loss, the Holy Spirit led me through that time and we were surrounded by godly men and women, to help mend us and build us back up together. It's been 12 years since that time and it's so much easier but the years have felt long. The questions and mistrust went deep but God healed my heart. He covered my suspicions and created a new foundation for our marriage. We now have four beautiful children: three boys and our last baby is a girl... God's redemption, timing, and presence has been undeniable!!

Gwyne, USA

My story would be a sum of ups and downs: of being with Jesus and running away from Him, of believing in lies and running away from my problems out of fear, and then running to Him again. But all of the time He was and is still with me, offering me mercy.

Ester, Slovakia

When I was 13 years old my innocence was stolen from me. It wasn't until I was older that I became aware of what I had been through. To me, it had always just been something that I was too embarrassed to tell others, something to keep quiet and hidden. One day I stumbled across a YouTube video of a woman sharing an experience just like mine, and I realised that I was a victim of sexual abuse. Being able to give a name to what had happened to me gave me a sense of comfort. I suddenly knew that I wasn't the only one to experience that pain, but the shame I felt about what had happened caused me to bury the memory and forget it was there.

Fast forward a few years to high school, where life is suddenly all about who's party you're going to at the weekend or whether you've 'done bits' with the boy you're snap chatting. At this time, I still believed that I was still a Christian. I was completely unaware of how far away from God I was. I would tell myself I believed in God but would deny it to anyone who asked me. I would pray, but in secret and only in times of need.

I was trapped in a physically, sexually, emotionally and spiritually abusive relationship for three years. When I look back all I see is darkness. A girl who just wanted to love and be loved, but had forgotten what love felt like.

I am praying that this prayer that I wrote may provide comfort for anyone who is learning to appreciate their own journey with God. Anyone who is trying to figure out this journey towards a life of fullness with our Good Father. We're in this together.

Lord, You were there in all my darkest moments.
You were with me even when I felt a million miles from you.

Maddie, UK

I didn't know it, but through all my suffering You were right there with me.
I was blind.
I was so lost.
I forgot what it felt like to know you.
Caught up in the world and putting my trust and identity in anyone but You.
And I was left feeling completely alone.

Time has passed and Lord You have brought me into a safe place.
But why don't I feel healed?
Why is my darkest moment still what defines me most?

Lord, I feel worthless.
I feel this is unacceptable.
Ashamed
Dirty.
Not worthy of love.
I long to feel pure.
To feel whole again.
To see me as Your beautiful creation.

Lord, I long to feel cleansed.
To feel white as snow.
To feel accepted.
But I can't shake off the identity that has defined me for so long.

Dirty, unacceptable, worthless.

I worry that my shame runs so deep that it will never disappear.
That it has been hidden for so long that I will never overcome it.

Maddie, UK

I've allowed my shame to become my identity.

I know you hold a path for me that leads away from shame and ends in acceptance and honour, but I just find it so hard to believe in my heart that there will be a day when I feel clean.

I feel close to You again.
I remember what it feels like to know You.
But still, I feel so far from You.
My shame builds a wall.
It stops me from seeing You as my Father.
Because I don't feel worthy of Your love, Your forgiveness, and Your acceptance.
Over and over, I ask myself:
How can such a perfect, loving God accept someone like me as His daughter?

I'm too dirty.
Too worthless.
Too broken.

I know of Your forgiveness, and that no sin is too great for You.
But I just can't comprehend it.

My heart still doesn't believe it.
Each day I see myself as someone who is broken.
But Lord, I also see someone who wants to heal.
To grow.
To learn.
To learn what Your love and forgiveness is.

Lord, I know that when I feel like ruins, You see foundations.

Maddie, UK

I don't want my failure to define me anymore. I want You to define me.

Lord use my failures, for Your power is made perfect in weakness.

May my weaknesses cause me to depend more on, and draw closer to you.

Lord, You have been so faithful in my life.
I feel like the wayward son who has returned home.
Lord, You were there when I felt I had strayed too far.
When I thought You wouldn't find me.

And You brought me home, back to the place I've always belonged.

Maddie, UK

When I was fourteen my dad died. He had cancer and it was a very tough time in his life. After this, I experienced depression and anxiety. Jesus has been a source of comfort and has challenged me to face the things that scare me.

Without Jesus, I don't know how I would have gotten through those times. He put me in the right place to get help and put the right people in my life to pull me out of the worst times. Even when I was yelling at Him and angry at Him, He stood by me and supported me in a way nobody else ever could.

Kate, UK

I knew how to be a 'Christian' and what that looked like. I found church boring and at the age of 14 refused to go anymore. I always intended to return to church but it was never the right time, and I enjoyed being a 'Christian' whilst living life my own way.

Being a Christian at that point for me looked like believing in God and praying sometimes. I suffered from severe anxiety as a teenager. I was depressed and at one point was thinking about taking my own life. This carried on into my young adult life and involved self-harming, low self-esteem and an emotionally abusive relationship.

I explored the idea that perhaps God wasn't real and it was all something I had just learnt as a child. I tried to believe He wasn't real but something inside me couldn't deny it and it was only 24 hrs of trying not to believe in Him before I couldn't ignore that He was real.

At the age of 21, I felt something was pulling me back towards Him without me really realising it. About a year later I told my boyfriend of 7 years that I wanted to try going back to church. I lived in London and he lived in the city of Brighton at the time. He found a church in Brighton and suggested we go. I got the feeling I had each time my sisters invited me to church. I wanted to go but as soon as it was mentioned something in me really pushed me back. Somehow I ended up going to church the following Sunday and I instantly felt like I was home. I felt awkward and uncomfortable being in a church but in my heart, I felt at home.

My boyfriend and I argued the next Sunday and he didn't want

Letitia, UK

to go again. Usually, the anxiety of going alone would have stopped me but something in me switched and I took myself there without him. I knew this was where I needed to be but I knew it was going to draw me away from my boyfriend, which scared me. I took some space from him and went to a festival. I felt like a fraud. I'd grown up in this environment and had gone to a Christian festival every year as a child but I felt like I didn't know anything about the Bible or Jesus. I felt like I was pretending and would get found out.

Whilst I was at the Christian festival I committed to getting to know Jesus and everyone around me was incredibly friendly and welcoming. I decided that I would start going to church every week and I travelled to the Brighton every Sunday from London. A few weeks later I broke up with my boyfriend. The relationship was unhealthy, emotionally abusive and exacerbated by anxiety.

My anxiety didn't disappear when I became a Christian. In some ways, it became harder because I no longer felt comfortable running away from all the things that scared me. I started to face things and do things that terrified me.

Life became uncomfortable in a new way. But I wasn't alone. I was comforted and strengthened by Jesus. He walked me through my fears and slowly their hold on me weakened, my panic attacks disappeared and my anxiety started to go. It's a big old journey and asking Jesus into my life is hands down the best thing I have ever done. I never want to go back to living without Him.

Letitia, UK

What is one thing you have learnt about Jesus?

Jesus is capable and able to carry what I can't. He can handle my anger, sadness, grief, disappointments, and hurt. He isn't shocked by it at all.

He is everything I truly want and need.

THAT HE IS SO LOVING!! There is nothing I can do that will make him love me any more or any less. We are so precious to him and his favourite thing is to hear from us and spend time with us. He is for us and he is so so good. He is full of grace, he always forgives and he has amazing plans for us all. We just have to step out in faith and trust him and he turns all things and makes them good. Even on the hard days, he is still there cheering us on and just because things are hard it doesn't mean he has forgotten about us, he is always there. There is purpose in every season.

Jesus is SO patient!!!

That He is everything.

That he is faithful.

He loves me no matter what.

He is so much fun! The number of times he surprises me, or fills my life with joyful things! He's just the best!!

He will never leave you. Never ever ever.

His love is so vast and we cannot do anything in our own strength but trusting in his strength means we can do all things!

Multiple people

What is one thing you have learnt about Jesus?

He's good and he's fun. He's good even when things feel bad. He's good when you don't get the things you want. And he's good when you do. He's knows best and as hard as it's been when life hasn't gone the way I'd hoped or planned he has always had better in mind.

He longs for a deep relationship and connection with us. He is abounding in love, and His grace and mercy is a free gift we don't need to earn and strive for. No sin is too big for Him to handle, He keeps no record of wrongs!

He is so faithful - He never ever runs away from us. If He feels distant it's because we have run from Him, never the other way around.

He is so good!! So good that's it's crazy. He's always championing us and no matter what happens He wants the best for us because we are so precious to Him!!

He is so gracious and just keeps pouring out his love on me even though I don't deserve it.

I'm not a good waiter, and I'm not good with the unknown! I like to know exactly what's going to happen, how, why and when so I can be totally prepared. But of course, God doesn't work like that! I'm really learning that His timing is perfect.

His forgiveness, peace and joy is beyond anything I could have imagined.

He never absolutely never gives up on us.

Multiple people

If I had to make a soundtrack of my childhood, 'Shine Jesus Shine' would be up there at numero uno. So my testimony isn't one of night and day, darkness to light. I guess I'd describe it more as a little light, always burning, but gradually getting brighter and brighter.

I got to year 10 when I began to realise there was actually a bit more to Christianity than I first thought... Surprise, surprise. After a youth weekend away with my church, I experienced the Holy Spirit in a way I never had before. It was a bit of an 'aha' moment. It wasn't anything crazy. I just felt the most over-whelming presence of God just resting on me and the other youth there. I started getting into the Bible, something I had hardly ever done before. The Bible is the only book which is physically LIVING. How epically cool and mind-boggling is that? Something my Nana says, which never fails to make me want to pick up the Bible, is that, 'Every. Single. Day. Jesus writes you a love letter, and it's just there waiting for you to pick it up and read it'. If you were sent a love letter, you'd want to read it, right?

I didn't have a very easy time at school. I was in one of those in-between groups. I was mates with the sporty girls, but also the academics, and my group fitted somewhere in the middle. From years 7-12, I was bullied pretty badly, it sort of seemed to follow me everywhere. I would be in one group and be the target, so I'd move to a different group and the same thing would happen over and over again. Thank Jesus, there were some people who were wonderful and I'm still friends with them. But I had a really difficult time constantly being picked on for my appearance, personality and everything in between. Pretty much, my identity was in shreds by the time I got to sixth form, and I

Kitty, UK

found it difficult to stay close to Jesus when I felt like I'd been through an emotional car wash over and over again for 6 years straight.

Naturally, over the years I developed a very complicated relationship with my mental health and fell into a whole lot of anxiety and depression. I had fallen into a pattern of comparing myself to everyone around me and trying to fit in and I came to the conclusion that I simply wasn't good enough. Little did I know, Jesus was about to swoop in and do what He always does: restore.

My mental health had taken a massive hit from lockdown - like a lot of other people. The big move to university in a new city and a new church all on my own was fast approaching and now I look back, the enemy was throwing all sorts of mental health-shaped obstacles in my way to try and stop me from going where the Lord wanted me! I had my heart set on Brighton, and before I had even got in, I felt a real sense of peace about it for some reason - I just knew that was where I would be going. I had every reason not to, but Jesus was so kind that He blessed me with peace.

Before I arrived in Brighton for uni I asked for a church, He blessed me with a new family and a church that felt like home from the first time I set foot inside. I asked for Christian friends, He blessed me with more friends than I can count - all of which, I know are lifelong friends. I asked for my mental health not to stand in my way, He blessed me with a new definition of who I am in Jesus and I have never been more peaceful.

Kitty, UK

My favourite moments have always come after a struggle when I've walked away from Him, tried to do things my own way and realised He has been by my side through it all. I fall back in love every time.

Lucy, UK

I feel so at peace knowing that God has plans to prosper me and that He will make my paths straight. I needn't worry about the future because He is holding me so closely. I also feel a sense of weightlessness and that I do not need to prove anything or be ashamed as I am representing the King of Kings. I feel like I've got a new identity and I am no longer a citizen of this world but rather, a citizen of heaven! Even little things, like worrying about my dog, I can just give over to Him and know that He has us in the palm of His hands.

Jesus is continually astounding me with His plans and works in my life. The beautiful Holy Spirit is truly incredible, as I feel like every day I get broken down only to be reconstructed and built back up as a child of the King. Times in my life that have made me fall more in love with Jesus have been when God has broken things off me and reminded me of my identity in Him. I feel so at peace knowing that God has plans to prosper me and that He will make my paths straight.

Emmeline, UK

I've been dealing with mental struggles since I was 8 years old, which became more severe throughout the years due to trauma. My youth was spent in therapy rooms, where I've been mistreated and was put under a lot of unhealthy pressure; scary things happened and the only thing that kept me going was music and my best friend. At the end of 2019 I hit a breaking point, at that point I had years of traumatic events and I was not getting the right treatment behind me. I gave up the hope that anything could help me and tried to live with it. I ignored all my fears, and all the unprocessed pain, and talked it down completely.

My boyfriend lent me his Bible. I started reading the Bible every morning, listening to worship songs and watching sermons and God's presence gave me a peace I had never known before. Things weren't all good from then on, trauma continued. But once I started praying and having hope that maybe there is hope, things started to change. So here I am... Mending and healing wounds, having faith and hope in a future full of beautiful things. I now have kindness and love around me, in the form of God's Love and love from the people around me. He continues to meet me where I'm at and I just know and trust that He will lead me towards beautiful things. You are never too far gone. Hope is never lost.

Mila, Germany

I know that I can go to God and He's always walking next to me, helping me move forward in school when I feel totally over-whelmed! He brings me so much peace and joy and helps me see the good in every situation!!

I became a Christian at a festival when I was 14, during a talk about saving yourself for marriage, of all things lol. I found myself praying on my knees, crying and feeling a love like I'd never felt. I'd grown up with quite atheist parents and I too was a firm non-believer. In an instant my heart posture changed, sadly my actions didn't but God has always been so kind and gracious and met me right where I am.

God clearly told me when I was at a house party about a year or two later that I was to remove myself from this environment and friendships and see what happens. I didn't have many friends for a while but God has taken me on many adventures since. Ten years later, I've had experiences I never dreamt of and have the absolutely dreamiest friends.

I'm so thankful for the embrace of Jesus wherever I may feel I get it wrong, He is so forgiving and I'm thankful for that. He never promised life will be easy and straightforward but I rest in the truth that He will walk with us and it will be worth it!

Bethany, UK

When I was 10 I developed an eating disorder and I had severe body dysmorphia, but I got some help and support from my parents and got a bit better. Then covid hit and I had anxiety, as well as major panic disorder, meaning I would have panic attacks on a daily basis. I had awful body image and anger issues and I was really struggling. I began self-harming as a coping mechanism and it hurt my relationship with my parents.

I lost my faith in God as I couldn't understand why I was going through all of this if He really loved me and was there for me. As my mental health began to improve, I still hadn't recovered my relationship with God. But then I went to a festival and I experienced God again through worship. I rediscovered my faith with a newfound passion and I returned as a completely changed person. I got baptised and I am so happy. I still have struggles but I am now learning to deal with them side by side with God.

Sophie, UK

I certainly have a much clearer sense of self and a clearer direction of where I am going now. I know it's not about me, it's all about Him! I couldn't imagine doing life without Him!

I struggled with anxiety. I felt alone, isolated and desperate. Looking back a few months, I remember feeling as though I was past the point of being helped. That anxiety was going to be my whole life, and that I should just get used to it. I didn't really want to speak about it at the time, I thought it was kind of embarrassing because, before it all happened, I was so flipping in love with Jesus! I kept thinking if I tell people I'm struggling they may relate it to my relationship with Jesus.

Now, however, I am more in love with Jesus than ever and I've grown really grateful for this difficult, messy period in my life because I can now remind myself of God's faithfulness, and help other people. So, thank you, Jesus, for my anxiety!!

Talking to people really helped me. When I spoke to someone about my anxiety at school, the weight was lifted off and I felt a glimpse of the freedom to come. I went home knowing this is going to be a long journey, requiring persistence. I remember saying to God, "if you are there, I'm in and I want to beat this". He has never left my side and He never will.

Now, I don't experience the same level of intense anxiety but there are times when I will feel overwhelmed and nervous, which is totally normal. I can say 'nerves be gone in Jesus' name' with full faith, and the feelings quickly go away!

Flo, UK

He loves me and loves to spend time with me and He will never leave me.

What is one thing that you would tell someone who doesn't know Jesus yet?

He is everything you are looking for.

Give it a go, you'll never regret it.

He died for you and He has a plan and a purpose for you.

You are not too messy or too broken or too… Anything for Jesus. In fact, You are so loved!!! I felt the exact same way once and I can assure you, He has seen you, He has known you for so long, and He has loved you for the longest time. He sees all of you and He just wants to love you and take all the things that feel heavy. He wants the things you feel like you can't even show him and He wants to make you whole again!!! So, if you're questioning taking that leap into faith… DO IT!!!!! There's so much love waiting for you on the other side.

Life with Jesus has nothing to do with religion; He wants a relationship. Accepting Jesus into your life doesn't mean you have to change and be a 'good' person, it means you accept your shortcomings and turn away from your old life and receive His free forgiveness, because He paid it all on the cross for you!

Ask Him and He will answer, He will reveal Himself to you. Someone once described God as a gentleman to me, He will not force His way on you, He won't push Himself on you, He will gently knock on the door of your heart, He will bring people into your life to share His word. He wants to come into your life, but only if you allow Him in.

He is freedom. What tastes like freedom in the world is actually super imprisoning but Jesus came to give us life and life to the full. He is the only way.

Multiple people

What is one thing that you would tell someone who doesn't know Jesus yet?

He's simply ready to be a friend of yours.

He's the best Father and friend, He is life-changing and life with Him is like going from black and white to colour!

He loves you so much, I could never put it into words. Even if you don't love Him, He still very much loves you.

I would tell them that it's not too late. There is a God who loves you more than you could ever comprehend. He wants to show you a new way to live and it's not too late to say yes to a life of wonder with Him.

Read the Bible and speak to someone who knows Him. He loves you more than you could ever imagine.

We all want to be seen, heard, and loved… And Jesus is the only one I have had faith in and have a relationship with, whom I know beyond a shadow of a doubt that I am deeply seen, unmistakably heard, and passionately loved and cared for by Him.

He loves you more than anything or anyone ever will. He sees you. He knows you. He knows what you've experienced and what you've tried to fill the voids with. He would love it if you'd come to Him just as you are and allow Him to hold you and forgive you, heal and transform you. He is so good. He is kind. Gentle. Merciful. Faithful. He is able to take on the mess in your life. Choose Him and experience life to the full.

If you don't know, get to know!!

You are so loved.

Multiple people

I first really encountered God when I went to my first camp at church. I remember it was in worship and I looked at the cross and I just burst into tears. I just felt a huge amount of love wash all over me and I knew that this could only be Jesus. I've had some rocks in my journey with Him and some had led me to fall away from Him, but some have brought me closer to Him. I feel like being a Christian is never just walking in a straight line: there are always gonna be points where you feel further away from Him or closer to Him.

He has helped me through a lot regarding my mental health and it really calms my anxiety to listen to worship music and just being in His presence. I think anybody who doesn't know God and the amazing love He has for us is definitely missing out!!

Issy, UK

I've loved God for most of what I can remember. I did a lot of things well growing up, for a long time, but I have pieces of my story that were broken. Life didn't go as perfectly as I grew up thinking and knowing it to go. I ended up married and divorced shortly into that marriage. Then I got pregnant out of wedlock, quickly married again, and had an annulment of that marriage within a short period of time. A lot of shame, guilt and brokenness set in. I had another pregnancy and eventually got married again. I have done a lot of healing, learning, and growing with Jesus. I got connected in discipleship and house churches and found out more of what I was uniquely and passionately created for.

Jesus has been connecting me with amazing friendships and deepening me beyond words. I feel the best is yet to come, even though it's taken years to get some things right. I love my family and love what we've created with our children. To God be the praise of the great things He has done!

Amy, USA

I was born in the 60s, with an abnormality in my spinal cord and I was diagnosed with Spina Bifida. At first, my parents were told that I would not walk and would either have to use a wheelchair or wear callipers on my legs and use crutches. At that time, my father applied for a new job, which took us to live in London. Under a new GP, my mother was told about a surgeon who was doing pioneering work on my type of Spina Bifida. I was sent to Great Ormond Street Hospital for sick children and underwent several operations in the next three years, followed by extensive periods of rehabilitation. The surgeries were eventually successful in enabling me to walk and run normally, for which I have always been incredibly grateful.

I was never taught anything about God. My father had various mental health challenges and my home was a mixture of him constantly being in rages, shouting and swearing, with mum constantly trying to appease him and calm him down. In fact, the only time I heard the name Jesus Christ was as a swear word.

A friend invited me to go to church with her family and I asked my parents if I could go. They said, 'no' because they didn't want me to be 'brainwashed'. I persisted however because I felt drawn to how my friend was describing the Church. Eventually, my parents said that I could go, but that if I started talking about it too much I would not be allowed to go again. I think mum again just wanted some peace and quiet for a little while as I was still so very clingy to her. I was happy to be allowed to go but quickly learned not to talk about it at home.

So, I started going along at the age of 8, very occasionally, to Catholic mass with my friend and her family. The years passed and I chose to go to a Catholic high school. We were taught by

Susan, UK

an order of nuns. One nun, in particular, took a special interest in me. At this point in my life aged 14-15, I was starting to despair of my father's constant unpredictable moods and seeming dislike of me, whilst my four years younger brother was showered with very obvious attention and praise.

My father constantly acted as though he hated me and, now that I was growing into a young woman, I was finding this very difficult to process. I still struggle, and although I was unable to verbalise any of this to this nun, she sensed that I was becoming withdrawn and depressed and really reached out to try and help me.

I spent a number of years not attending any church. I left home at 17, married at 19 and had my first baby at 23. I had a lovely group of friends who I met through a playgroup run by a group of mothers from a local Anglican church. It was after the birth of my second child, and after experiencing a terrible postnatal depression which made me question everything about life, that I eventually became a Christian by kneeling down beside my bed, saying, 'sorry' to God for how I had been over the years and inviting Him into my life to take spiritual charge of me. Over the next few weeks, I felt an incredible level of peace. I was eventually baptised. I know that God is for me, not against me and that I will never face disappointment alone.

Susan, UK

I grew up in a Christian home but I'm the kind of person who has to decide things for myself. I only went to church as a teen because I had loads of friends there. Christianity didn't really resonate with me, even though I had no doubt there was a God. I experienced a lot of life at a young age: got kicked out of a few schools, got into trouble, drugs, binge drinking, and wasn't up for the church thing at all anymore.

I discovered for myself this was fun for a while and then it suddenly became quite a dark and empty road. It attracted a lot of spiritual warfare, fear and nightmares. I actually needed Jesus.

There came a point one day when I was looking in the mirror and I felt totally empty after a festival where my friends and I had been on drugs all weekend partying. My eyes were lifeless and I just knew I needed Jesus. I gave my life to Him a few days later alone on the beach, sitting on a rock!

I walked away from the environment I was in and dove straight into an internship at a church. A few months later, I encountered God in my bedroom. I saw a vision of the cross and just knew Jesus had died for me. I was genuinely sorry for all the wrong I had done. I left my bedroom to see the world from black and white to colour - from spiritually dead to spiritually alive. And the rest is history!

Rae, UK

My life before Jesus lacked meaning and purpose. I struggled a lot with anxiety, social anxiety, and my mental health which I believe has greatly improved since giving my life to Jesus and trusting Him and His plan for me. I feel so grateful for life and so excited to grow my relationship with Him. I truly believe that He has helped with my struggles.

Imogen, UK

When I joined secondary school I was exposed to a lot that I wasn't used to or comfortable with. I got much busier and became someone who would almost live two separate lives of church and school. My family prayed a lot with me as church couldn't go ahead, so I no longer had that in my life. I started to pray less and less by myself, becoming only a crutch for me in extreme circumstances, and I found myself only talking to God when I had problems.

I started getting myself into difficult situations with some guys in my life, where I decided not to turn to God or anyone else for many decisions I was making. I thought I could take everything on myself, I thought I could manage difficult situations myself, with my own judgement and when things didn't work out I felt like a failure. I drifted further away from God and further away from myself. When it all became too much, I was angry at God for letting me and others get so hurt and constantly asked the question, "why God?".

I started to open up and pray again and God reminded me that He's been with me the whole time - all I needed to do was ask for His help and reach out to Him, for He wants me to be my Father and my friend and He knows what's best for me. God wants to connect with you because He loves and cares about you.

Since rebuilding my relationship with God, He's reminded me of the power of prayer, especially the significance of praying for others as well as myself.

Raffy, UK

Well, I've been a part of a Christian family my whole life, but I used to go to church just because my mom and dad made me. I didn't like going to church, I didn't feel like I belonged. I was 14 back then and I thought to myself, "I always wanted to get baptised at this age, but now I don't even see the point, I don't even think God has a plan for me".

One night, after I finished my classes, my brother picked me up as always. It seemed like a normal Tuesday, but what little did I know. I got into the car and some song was playing, I don't know if I had heard it before. It was the song, 'Living Hope', playing in our Romanian version. We have a part where the singer says, "Jesus, You have set me free". The moment I heard that I felt like some chains had broken and like I was free, I started crying and when I got home I went straight to my room and I prayed like I never did before. And I said, "Jesus, if you really have a plan for me, just do it your way and guide me there". I waited a couple of months, and a friend of mine asked me to come with her to the church. At first I hesitated, but I went anyway.

Before I went, I prayed, "Jesus, if you have a plan for me, show me tonight somehow". I got there and the first thing the pastor said was, "We have a baptism coming on the 1st of march". My birthday was coming up, and so I got baptised, and I was really amazed. Ever since God has worked in my life in ways I can't express.

Lori, Romania

I was born with a severe heart disease called Cardiomyopathy. I was then held in the hospital for some days for every scan you can imagine. The doctors weren't sure whether I was going to make it, but as you have probably worked out... I made it.

I first became aware of God when I was 7! I know, super young. You could argue that a 7-year-old can't hear or feel something like that, but I definitely felt a super strong presence and warmth that I'd never felt before. The exact date was 10-10-2010, I was down the front at my church with a colouring sheet in my hands. My grandpa was the pastor of the church at the time and was handing the church down to my auntie. I just remember so clearly feeling so loved and overwhelmed, and hearing His voice so clearly that it was something so different to anything I had ever heard before. I said, "Please God, can you come into my life?", and in that moment my eyes instantly started to well up and I could do nothing but cry. For the rest of that day, all I could think about was what this new craze and passion that had inhabited in my heart. I couldn't get this off my mind. I ran straight up to my room after church and quickly wrote everything down.

Looking back, I can see both the blessings and the challenges of growing up Christian. There were many times when it felt like an uphill battle and many times I felt like I wasn't enough or would doubt myself regularly. But through it all, my faith definitely saved me from many things. My faith grew stronger in the things I saw and felt.

I saw actual miracles happen in front of my own eyes. People with paralysed bodies are getting up from their wheelchairs and running around; people are being completely changed through the simple act of inviting Jesus into their lives.

Levi, UK

Another yearly hospital scan for my heart condition was due, and there was my mum and I back again waiting for the same bad news or conversation. This day was not one to forget as we left that hospital on that day with news that they were completely shocked to find out that my condition was completely off the scales of being normal and undiagnosable. They did not know why or how, but my mum and I had an idea who it was. Only now do I look back on this time and thank God every day for this news. The significance of this story continues to amaze me.

Fast forward a few years, I started to love the art of guitar and this quickly became my new escape and favourite hobby. I fell in love with the instrument. My first guitar was given to me by another guy who was playing at this Christian conference. He was playing the exact guitar I'd dreamed of having: same colour, same spec, same everything. At the end of the week I approached him to compliment him on his guitar playing, and he felt as if the Lord at the moment told him to give me his guitar because he could sense an anointing on my life with the guitar. I was in a mess. A happy mess. This was another stepping stone moment to outline my calling.

I believe God has called me to play music and inspire people, and to be a servant of His love. I went through college and then spent a year doing an internship at my local church, which brought me many life-long friends and taught me a lot. God has been super kind about the simple things in my life, for which I'll be forever grateful for.

We all have a story. We all have a Testimony.
He turns our mess into a Message.

Levi, UK

I grew up knowing about God and Jesus. Church was tradition for me and I thought Christianity was about being a good religious girl. As a teen, I distanced myself from God. However, I also attended Christian youth camps where young adult leaders would give up a week of their summer to get alongside awkward teenagers and show them Jesus.

I was one of those awkward teens, and after going to a few of these camps, I realised the significance of the Gospel message and what Jesus did for me. One year, something changed. I knew that Jesus had died for me. Even though I didn't deserve it. I didn't really know how to live as a Christian after this. But I knew I wanted to keep Jesus in my life, not just at church on a Sunday.

As I became an adult and went off to uni, I was blessed to find a welcoming church which helped me to live out my faith as a young adult. Life has not been easy since following Jesus, but it has been better because I have a certain hope for the future that cannot be shaken and a friend in Jesus who will never let me down.

Zoe, UK

I wasn't wanted. My parents didn't get on and their relationship was toxic. Had I been born these days I would have been taken away from them. My life was one of abuse. My mum had anger issues but as I got older I began to understand where the anger came from. My father was a nasty man. To be honest I didn't love him at all. I had zero confidence and very few friends, he didn't allow me to have them.

When I was 14 I went to a concert with a Christian friend and I found Jesus. That made my dad angry. I went to church with my friends and it was there I found out what a proper family was. They spoke to me kindly, cherished me, and made me feel worthwhile.

By the time I was 20 I had to turn my back on the church. I really couldn't cope with my father anymore. At 21 I took myself to Canada for a while and I came back as a different girl.

I had made an application to immigrate there, I had accommodation and a job organised but the day I came back from Canada he started again. At dinner, he started banging the table and ranting and raving at me, telling me how ugly, stupid and worthless I was. He also stole my address book so I couldn't contact anyone in Canada.

I turned to drink and drugs. To escape him, I married a man I didn't love. Which wasn't fair but I really tried to make the marriage work. 14 years down the line I left. I was sick of the way he treated me, sick of the nasty way he treated my daughter and sick of his drinking. Shortly after I re-married my ex-husband. I stayed with my ex-husband as my only alternative was going back to live in a house with my father.

Mari, UK

I found my way back to a church. The pastor there was great and helped me to get back on my feet and encouraged me to go to university. He and his wife were so proud of me when I graduated. My mum died just after my graduation and I got left to look after my dad on my own.

To be honest I resented every second I had to spend with him. I couldn't work because of his unreasonable demands on my time. Seven days a week I had to see him and not just that, I got into considerable debt because of it.

When he died I didn't grieve and I struggled with that, but a very good Christian friend helped me. She said that we are told to, "honour your father and mother" and I had done that by looking after someone who deliberately caused me so much harm, and by honouring my father I had honoured God. I still have some bad days but I get through them. There are times when I find it hard to pray but at the very least I say thank you to Jesus for all He has done for me and I know He's beside me every step of the way.

Mari, UK

I grew up in a Christian family that loved God and the Church. As I grew older it became apparent that this faith was a foundation for all the lives that I loved so dearly. I loved that they would talk about Jesus when it came to almost everything. I realised, "Wow! They really are living for something bigger".

So, I decided at 9 years old that I wanted to give my life away to something so much greater than little me. I committed my life to God the day before my ninth birthday. I ran downstairs to tell my dad. He replied, "Inds, that's amazing! Did you ask him to forgive you for your sins?". I had forgotten that bit. Without saying anything, I ran upstairs back to the same part of my beige carpet and said, "Lord forgive me for my sins", opened my eyes and ran back downstairs for breakfast.

Since that moment, I have been sold out for Jesus. That might sound like a very uncool thing to say for some of you, but it's the greatest thing I've ever done. I've never lived a day in my life unsure of why I am here. Faithful is actually my middle name (no joke) and I believe that sticking with Jesus was a big reason I got through my teenage years more sure of why I am here and who I am. It was in my teenage years that I had many more questions about faith, as my mind began to try and comprehend what I had accepted as a young girl.

I went to a youth camp with my friends one year and the leader asked for any people in the room who felt called to speak to generations to stand up. Out of nowhere, I felt something so deep in the pit of my stomach that just felt like the urge to stand up. So there I was, the first to stand in front of a crowd of thousands of youth, legs shaking, eyes closed, pretending that I'm just on my own in my bedroom. Then, an eruption of applause began, and

Indi, UK

as I opened my eyes I could spot the thirty-odd other youth also standing with me, who felt that same deep pit in their stomach. A rush of what I now know was the Holy Spirit was felt within me. I started feeling it in my hands and they started to uncontrollably shake, then my legs started to give in and tears were rolling down my cheeks as I felt this weird and indescribable feeling of being so known and so loved.

From that moment on I knew I could not deny what I had felt and what so many people around me so faithfully devoted their lives to. Since then, my life has been devoted to God's call on my life to speak and I believe that He has a perfect plan for me and will guide my steps in life, not for the desires of the world, but for His.

Growing up both my parents knew and loved God. I loved going to church as a kid and really believed God was real and I knew He loved me. I think that was hugely impacted by how my parents and people from church loved me.

I don't think it's a coincidence that God sent His Son as a human, to show us who He is. God loves to remind us of who He is through people (the best example of this is Jesus), but He really used people I looked up to at church: parents, godparents, etc, to display part of His love and affection for me in my childhood.

When I was 8 my mum was diagnosed with cancer which then progressed over four years before she passed away when I was 12. This was a really confusing but equally foundational time for my faith. I really, really thought my mum would be healed by God and I completely believed this was possible. When she died I felt really angry and hurt by God, "Why would you be able to heal her, and even convince me that you would, but not follow through with that?". It was a dark time but I still loved church and wanted to be there, especially when I was feeling my worst. I never stopped believing in God but I did feel so angry and let down by Him. It was a big few years of working out what I believed about him.

He has taught me so much about Him through not having my mum here. He has also taught me it's okay when it's hard and I can't see what good has come from my hardship. It's okay because He has everything under control.

Emma, UK

We are afflicted in every way, but not crushed; perplexed, but not driven to despair; persecuted, but not forsaken; struck down, but not destroyed.

2 Corinthians 4:7-11

Jesus, we love you and we are so grateful for you.

We thank you that you love us at our worst
and you love us at our best.
You have never failed to give us all that
we need at the right time.

We thank you that you are a redeeming, loving, patient,
kind and fun father who is always working
behind the scenes for us.

We thank you that your plans and desires for us are
stronger than those of the enemy.
May you help us to hear your voice and be more aware
of your presence in our everyday lives.

We praise you.
We love you.
We need you.

Amen

Hey there,

I hope you feel encouraged after reading this book!

Isn't Jesus totally amazing and incredible?
He is the greatest friend you will ever have!

If you don't have a relationship with Jesus and would love to do life with Him, He would love that. At the end of the day, all the Christian stuff is just about having a relationship with Jesus and working out life with Him, not on your own.

If at some point you would love to give your life to Jesus I encourage you to read this prayer aloud. This is the best decision you will ever make.
You won't regret it.
Wahoooo!

Giving my life to Jesus prayer:

Lord Jesus, thank you for dying on the cross for me,
I'm sorry for the wrong things I've said and done,
Please forgive me and fill me with your Holy Spirit,
I invite you in and will follow you for the rest of my life,
Amen

Helpful things to get you started:

Order yourself a Bible:
You won't regret it, it's the greatest book ever written.
You will learn so much about Jesus.

Suggested versions:
ESV, CSB, NIV, Message

Get stuck into a Church Community:
A place where you can be encouraged in your faith.

This is how the Bible is formatted:
Matthew (book name) 11 (chapter) 28-30 (verses)

Bible stories/Books to read:
The Gospels - The Books are in the New Testament,
which include accounts of Jesus's birth, life on earth, death,
resurrection, his teachings and his miracles.

Matthew:	Mark:
Matthew 6:25-34	Mark 5:21-43
Matthew 14:22-33	Mark 6:30-44

Luke:	John:
All of Luke 2	John 4:1-26
Luke 7:36-50	John 18 onwards

Old Testament stories:
(Stories of what happened before Jesus was born)

1 Samuel 17
Daniel 3
Exodus 14:5-31
Genesis 1-3
Psalms 139 & 23
Proverb 3:5-6

If you'd like to share your experience with this book please feel free to email: *hello@testimonybook.org*
I would love to hear from you!

Jesus loves you a lot.

Printed in Great Britain
by Amazon

17751444R00082